Blessings

Transforming My Vietnam Experience

Don Yost

Sheed & Ward
Kansas City

Sheed & Ward™ is a service of The National Catholic Reporter
Publishing Company.

———————————◆———————————

Library of Congress Cataloguing-in-Publication Data

Yost, Don, 1945-
    Blessings : transforming my Vietnam experience / Don Yost.
      p.   cm.
    ISBN: 1-55612-804-5 (pbk. : alk. paper)
    1. Vietnamese Conflict, 1961-1975--Personal narratives,
American. 2. Vietnamese Conflict, 1961-1975--Psychological
aspects. 3. Yost, Don, 1945-   . I. Title.
    DS559.5.Y66   1995
    959.704'38--dc20   95-24018
                                        CIP

———————————◆———————————

Published by: Sheed & Ward
                  115 E. Armour Blvd.
                  P.O. Box 419492
                  Kansas City, MO 64141-6492

To order, call: (800) 333-7373

Cover design by Gloria Ortiz.

Contents

Dedicated with my deepest love
to Janie
my most cherished "Blessing"

To Michele and Dave
with fatherly love
to help you understand . . .

Foreword

Why I Wrote "Blessings"

Dear Michele and Dave,

Like the old sailor in *The Rhyme of the Ancient Mariner,* I have a story that I need to tell you. The story began in 1968 with my tour of duty in Vietnam and it will continue for the rest of my life.

It is a story of despair and hope. It is a story of hate and love, and it is a story of disillusionment and faith. In short, it is the story of living.

You see, everyone has some sort of "Vietnam" in their life. "Vietnams" are those things that make you feel alienated and bitter; those things that make you feel angry and those things that make you feel guilty.

Your "Vietnams" are very powerful motivators. The way you respond to them determines your future and defines who you are as a person. They have the ability to destroy you if you allow them to. They also have an immense power to force you to grow. If you use that power, if you channel it properly, it will help you to accomplish things you never thought possible.

I wish you didn't have to have "Vietnams" in your lives. I wish you didn't have to experience the hurt they bring. But they will come — they will come in spite of all my wishes — and they have much to teach you.

Use the wisdom you acquire from them to grow and, most importantly, use it to help other people. If you do this, you will come to see your "Vietnams" not only for what they are, but for what you can make of them.

The best gift a father can offer his children is the benefit of his experience. And so, I invite you to take this journey with me. I want to share my story with you . . . to tell you what I've learned of life.

Most of all, I've learned how much we need to be loved. If not for Mom's love, Vietnam would have destroyed me. It's her love that sustains me and it's within her love that I find the courage . . . the courage I've needed to change my "Vietnams" into — blessings.

Love, Dad

Blessings

Chapter One

"Nothing Left to Give"

"Fly the ocean in a silver plane . . .
Watch the jungle when it's swept with rain.
Just remember 'til you're home again . . .
You belong to me."

God, I was missing her. The words of our song, the one we danced to at our wedding, ran through my mind as I waited for sunrise.

The rain was heavier now and I couldn't see much farther than the barrel of the M-16 I aimed toward the tree line.

The monotonous beating of raindrops hitting my helmet was broken by the crack of distant small arms fire. "Somebody's getting hit," I thought in a detached, matter-of-fact sort of way. It didn't matter.

Nothing seemed to matter much anymore.

I didn't know the names of the guys lying there in the mud on either side of me. "Moe," "Goody," "Lefeaver," and the rest of my squad, all the guys I'd known since I'd been in the field — had been blown away that morning by a booby-trapped 105mm artillery shell.

I was only out of the field for a few hours. I went to Chu Lai to set up an allotment for Janie and when I got back, they no longer existed.

I recalled that morning as if it had happened in another lifetime.

Something was coming in over the field radio when I got back to "LZ Bronco."

"Get that goddamn dust-off in here . . . Now!"

The voice of the crackling radio transmission was frantic.

"What happened?" I asked the guys huddled around the radio.

"Charlie Company, 1st platoon . . . They hit a 105."

1

"Did you say 1st platoon?"

"Yeah."

"Oh Shit! Which squad?"

"Don't know, but it's bad. Hey, ain't that your platoon?"

They turned from the radio and stared at me, waiting for my answer. I felt like Peter being confronted after Jesus' arrest. "Surely you are one of them . . ."

I didn't have to answer. The "whup-whup-whup" of its blades told us a helicopter was coming in. We ran to the landing pad and got there just as the chopper set down.

I shielded my eyes from the dust and when I was able to see again, rucksacks were being thrown from the chopper's open door.

I looked inside and saw Little John struggling with the equipment. We called him "Little John" because he was barely 18 and he still looked like a little kid.

"What happened?" I shouted. He turned toward me.

Could this be the kid I was with just a few hours ago out in the field? It couldn't be. He looked too old.

"Little John, is that you?"

There was no expression. He was numb. The dirt on his face was smudged under his eyes where he had rubbed it with his sleeve. He'd been crying.

The chopper's blades were silent now.

"Goody's dead and Doc's takin' it really bad," he said.

He handed me a rucksack. When I grabbed it, my hand stuck to it. It was wet. Its drab, olive green color had turned to a strange, dark shade of maroon.

The words "Make Love Not War" were printed on it in pen with a peace sign forming the "o" in "Love."

"Oh, shit —" It was Dave's pack.

I dropped it on the pile with the others. Everything was maroon. Everything was covered with blood.

I helped Little John climb out of the chopper. It was an effort for him. His left pant leg was slit open, he wore only one boot and there was a dirty bandage wrapped around his ankle. He threw himself down next to the pile of bloody rucksacks.

Sitting there, slumped on the ground with his head down, he looked like one of them, like he belonged there in the pile, . . . part of the testament.

He shook his head slowly back and forth and he was moaning.

"Oh Man, everybody got hit . . . Doc . . . Poor Doc."

"Doc? . . . What happened to Doc?" I asked as I grabbed him by the shoulders to shake an answer out of him.

Doc was our medic. Everybody liked "Doc." He would do anything for you. He was a round, freckled-faced kid with thick, wire-rimmed glasses and red hair. He always smiled.

When he was able to speak again, Little John's words tumbled out of him as if the story would go away if he told it quickly.

"Lefeaver was walking point. He hit a 105. Everybody started screaming.

"Doc ran up to help and saw Goody sitting there on the ground. He ran past him. He didn't know Goody was hit too. He kept running from one guy to the next, trying to help them. Shit . . . they were all screaming, they just kept screaming . . ."

"What about Doc?" I asked him again.

"When he got back to Goody, he saw a trickle of blood on his shirt. Goody was hit bad, he got shrapnel in his heart. Doc was holding him, and . . ."

"And . . . what?"

Little John started to cry. His whole body shook with each sob. I put my arm around his shoulders to try to comfort him like an older brother. It wasn't the first time I'd felt that way. They saw me as an older brother. I was 23 and had graduated from college . . . an old man in Vietnam. Most of these kids were 18, 19 maybe, and fresh out of high school.

Little John wiped his eyes with his sleeve.

"And Goody died." he said. "He died in Doc's arms."

I felt a lump form in my throat and my eyes started to fill.

"Doc's blaming himself. He thinks it's all his fault," Little John said.

"Where's Doc now?"

"They sent him back with the dust-off."

"Damn it! Goddamn this place!" I thought. Why did Doc have to go through this? It was too much to ask of a good kid who never hurt anybody.

Little John had stopped crying now.

"What's his name, uh, Marshall? Yeah, Marshall. He got hit right in the stomach. They have to send him to Japan . . . Doc said it's too bad for them to fix him here."

Marshall always walked behind me on patrol. That meant he was in my spot when they hit the booby trap. It should have been me.

"What about Moe?" I asked.

A smile slowly appeared on Little John's face.

"He got hit in the legs, but Doc told him everything was O.K. It didn't hit anything important. Moe said that's all that mattered. Can you believe that? He said 'that's all that matters.' It was almost funny."

Moe was our squad leader. He looked black, his skin was so dark, but he was a short, skinny Puerto Rican from New York.

They came with a stretcher to carry Little John to the aid station. He looked at me before they took him away and I put my hand on his shoulder.

"Take care, O.K.?"

As they carried him off, I knew I'd never see him again.

The guys who ran down to the chopper with me were rummaging through the pile of rucksacks looking for personal effects.

I guessed the stuff would find its way back to its owners if they were alive, or back to their families if they weren't.

There were cherished letters from home that had been carried for months out in the field and pictures of smiling wives and girlfriends. There were carefully wrapped pieces of cookies left from mom's last "Care package" from home and pictures of Pontiac GTOs clipped from magazines.

One guy reached for Dave's pack, the one with the peace sign drawn on it and opened it.

Dave! . . . I didn't ask Little John about Dave.

He was a blonde-haired "Flower Child" from L.A. All he talked about was how he'd go surfing when he got back to "The world."

The guy who opened his pack, reached inside and pulled out a small plastic bag.

"Oh man, look what I found!" he shouted to the others. He was smiling.

"He won't be needin' this anymore!"

He put the bag in his shirt pocket.

"What the hell are you doing?" I asked him. "You can't keep any of this stuff."

"Says who? You don't want him gettin' in trouble do you?"

"No."

"Well then; shut the fuck up!"

He went back to digging through the pack.

It was sick, talking about Dave "getting in trouble." There was his rucksack, covered with blood. He was in trouble enough already. What would they do to him for smoking pot anyway? Send him to Vietnam?

I stood back and watched them for a moment. They were vultures, looking for anything that was of value to them, like the centurians casting lots at the foot of the cross.

I walked away disgusted.

"Who gives a shit anyway? . . . Don't mean nothin'!"

The thought seemed to comfort me.

It was time to go back to the field and I needed to get my rucksack and ammunition. When I walked through the door of the supply bunker, they were opening Goody's dufflebag and it fell over with a dull thud. A framed picture of his wife crashed to the floor.

They had been married right before Goody went to Vietnam, just like me and Janie.

"She's a very pretty girl," I thought.

As she smiled up at me through the shattered glass, I wondered how she would look with her heart broken.

I got my rucksack and ammunition and walked outside where it was easier to breathe. I needed to be alone.

I found an empty bunker, went inside where no-one would see me and sat down in the dirt. The sun's rays shining through the window reminded me of a church.

Sitting there with my arms folded across my knees, looking down at the ground, I thought about "Goody" and his wife.

I thought about me and Janie.

I thought about my whole squad being gone.

I thought about the war protesters and the kids who went to Canada to avoid the draft.

I thought about America and I thought about the Vietnamese.

And I cried silently . . . for all of us.

The sound of the helicopter's engine called me. It was time to go. I put on my steel pot, picked up my rifle and rucksack and started walking slowly toward the Huey.

"You'd better get your damn ass on that Chopper!"

"Like I've got a choice," I thought.

I stopped and looked in the direction of the voice.

"I'm doing that . . . Sir!" I yelled back at him.

I climbed into the Huey and sat cross-legged on its metal floor holding my rifle across my knees. The chopper was empty except for the two guys who would fly it and the door gunner. Their backs were toward me. I couldn't see their faces. They didn't seem human. They were just part of the machinery. Their round helmets made them look strange, like creatures from another planet. I looked out of the open door as the Huey lifted from the ground.

Vietnam looked peaceful from a distance. Yellow grass huts were surrounded by rice paddies divided into squares like lush, green checkerboards. Vietnamese dressed in their black pajama-like outfits labored in the heat under the clear blue and white sky, their heads protected from the sun by their pointed, coolie hats. Their trousers were rolled up to their knees as they waded in the rice paddy water. Their plow was a pointed log pulled by a huge, black water buffalo.

They had lived this way for centuries and it seemed right somehow; the way it was meant to be. Why couldn't it just be left alone? I was an intruder watching them through the open helicopter door; like a time traveler discovering an ancient civilization.

I felt the Huey bank to the right and begin its descent. I grabbed my rucksack and moved closer to the door to see what was left of Charlie Company.

They were on a hilltop getting ready to move out. The chopper landed and I ran out from under its rotating blades with my head down. When I looked up, I found myself in a different world.

I didn't recognise anyone. They were total strangers. No-one spoke. It was the eerie silence that comes from trauma and fear. Their unfamiliar faces were pale . . . zombies going through the motions of living . . . mourners at a wake . . . They had seen it happen.

"Where were you?" their pathetic eyes asked.

They made me feel dirty, standing there, the only one wearing clean fatigues . . . an outsider.

The silence was broken by a single word: "Yost!"

How did they know my name?

There was no way they could possibly know my name. It sounded different, like it didn't belong to me.

The black sergeant pointed to a hill in the distance across an open field of knee-high brush and looked directly into my eyes. He didn't say anything. He didn't have to . . . I was going to "Walk point."

There were more booby traps out there . . . waiting.

I would have to walk out in front of everybody else and "find" them.

"But I'm a college graduate. . . ." The ridiculous thought came and went in the same instant.

I clicked off the safety on my rifle, pulled the heavy rucksack higher on my shoulders and started walking . . . quickly.

I wanted it to end one way or another. I just wanted to get it over with. I didn't feel any emotion at all — no fear, no concern, no sense of personal danger. It was strange. I didn't even look for trip wires. It didn't matter. I was getting used to feeling like a piece of meat in this God-forsaken place.

The brush made a whooshing sound with each step as it hit against the legs of my pants, reassuring me that I was still alive. Sweat began pouring down my face and the salt made my eyes burn. My finger was tight on the trigger, . . . as if it would make any difference.

After a few minutes I glanced back over my shoulder to see if the others were keeping up. They weren't. They knew better. They stayed far behind, safe from the spray of shrapnel and blood they were expecting to see at any second. I was way out ahead of them by myself; all alone in my own private Vietnam.

I found myself at the top of the hill, not knowing how I'd gotten there, stumbling and gasping for breath like a runner at the finish line. With a groan, I pulled off the heavy pack and let it drop. I fell down next to it and lay there on the ground trying to breathe. My stomach muscles tightened suddenly and a sharp pain in my gut forced me to sit up. It felt like somebody was pushing a knife into me and twisting it.

Charlie Company was snaking its way through the open field below me. They were wide open. "A sniper could, . . . Ugh." The pain was worse.

I wrapped both arms around me and rocked back and forth. I felt my stomach heave, leaned to one side and vomited. Nothing came up. There was nothing left. I had nothing left to give.

Chapter Two

"A Suitable Ransom"

The open "Gook sores" on my arms itched and brought me back to the night ambush. Maybe the rain would help them. They never seemed to heal. Nobody knew what caused them; they just came with being a "Grunt."

"See the jungle when it's swept with rain." The words repeated themselves. I was missing Janie . . . badly.

It wasn't just loneliness; it was an aching, broken-hearted feeling mixed with guilt.

Why was I in Vietnam, anyway? She deserved better than this. We were supposed to be starting our lives together. Instead, my ass was in a rice paddy in Southeast Asia, thousands of miles away from her, and it was my fault — I didn't get drafted, I'd actually signed up. How incredibly dumb could I have been?

The guy on my left couldn't have been more than 19 but he looked years older. Being out in the field did that to people.

The slow, back and forth motion of the starlight scope he was looking through suddenly stopped. He must have seen something.

He put down the scope, picked up a hand grenade and pulled its pin. He waited a second before he threw it into the darkness in front of us, and ducked down behind the two-foot high rice paddy dike, waiting for the explosion.

"I hope he knows what the hell he's doing," I thought, as I put my head down. You weren't supposed to give your position away on night ambush until you saw the V.C.

The grenade exploded. "Now all of Southeast Asia knows where we are," I mumbled to myself.

He grabbed another grenade and threw it after the first.

"Oh shit . . . there must be something out there."

I peered over the dike and squinted into the darkness.

9

I saw the claymore mines we'd set out earlier. They looked innocent enough, like Polaroid cameras waiting for someone to happen by to have their picture taken.

The second grenade exploded.

I ducked behind the dike again as I saw his arm go back and start forward. A moment passed before I felt the explosion behind me. My left leg whipped at the knee from the concussion and I heard the guy on my right yell.

The kid who had been throwing the grenades looked over at me with a blank, stupid expression on his face.

I kept my rifle pointed at the tree line expecting the V.C. to appear at any second.

A minute or two passed before the black sergeant crawled over next to me.

"I've got three grenades and about eighty rounds of ammunition," I whispered.

I was giving him an inventory, like they taught us in Basic. But he wasn't listening.

"The claymores are set out, and . . . Ugh."

I felt a dull ache deep in my left foot, like a bad toothache.

"You one of the guys that got hit?" he asked in a disgusted tone of voice.

"Yeah."

"Get the fuck over here."

He took me back to the center of the perimeter.

"Sit your ass down here."

A kid who must have been their medic ran over to me. He looked at the blood oozing from my left boot and stared at me. His eyes widened. He was scared.

"Oh shit!" he said, and started digging frantically through his pack, throwing things on the ground. Finally he found a knife and cut the boot. As he pulled it off, blood ran out of it and a white hot pain shot up my leg.

"Oh Man! This is really bad! Bring that radio over here!"

I was glad my old squad didn't have this guy for our medic. "Doc" would have known what to do but this kid didn't, and he started to panic.

He didn't say a word to me. He was too wrapped up in his own problem and seemed annoyed that I'd put him in this situation.

He grabbed the field radio and started yelling for a dust-off.

"Sir! . . . Come in, Sir! . . . I need a dust-off in here right away! This guy is hurt bad! . . . His foot is . . . It's bad, Sir! . . . Come in, Sir. Can you hear me? I need a dust-off! . . . Sir?"

The Captain's voice came back over the radio. He must have been sleeping.

"What's your fuckin' problem?"

"I need a dust-off Sir. This guy's hurt bad."

"What happened?"

"He got hit with a grenade, Sir —"

"Beautiful! Just fucking beautiful!"

"I need a dust —"

"I can't send a fuckin' dust-off in there now!"

"But Sir, he's gonna lose his foot if we don't get him outta here. It's swelling up."

"A dust-off will give away your position! It'll fuckin' wait until morning!"

"But, Sir —"

"But nothin'! It'll wait, damnit!"

"But Sir . . . Sir?"

He was whimpering into a dead radio.

I didn't understand. The grenades had already given away our position. Unless "Charlie" was deaf and blind, he knew exactly where we were. I was going to lose a foot thanks to the captain's distorted logic.

But a sense of well-being suddenly came over me. It was perverted, like everything else in this Alice in Wonderland place where good was bad and bad was good. All Vietnam would cost me was a foot, . . . just a foot! They would cut it off and I could go home. I'd be of no further use to them. It would be worth it.

I fought back a sly smile . . . a gambler at a poker table trying to keep a straight face after being dealt an ace.

They thought the foot was of great value to me, a suitable ransom. They didn't know my father had lost his leg in World War II and that I had grown up with his artificial leg and stump socks.

"Amputee" was not a frightening word for me. It was another word for "Hero."

I glanced at my foot. It had swollen to twice its normal size and had turned an ugly, deep shade of purple. Dark blood was running from a hole on top of it and was trickling down between the toes. It was — beautiful!

My Vietnam would be over soon. Even the rain had stopped.

The medic put down the radio handset and took a syringe from his pack. He stuck the needle into the foot and the throbbing pain slowly went away.

Like a bad plumber trying to fix a leaking pipe, he worked in silent confusion.

He no longer cared. He tied a field dressing around the leak, and gave up.

"Good enough," he said to himself as he gathered his tools.

We both knew it wasn't "good enough." The lady of the house would be upset when she came home to see what he had done. The pipe was still leaking.

I picked myself up and hobbled over to where the black sergeant was sleeping. I sat down a few feet away from him to wait for morning and the dust-off. It would be a long night.

I was beginning to get nervous. What if the gooks really were out there getting ready to come in after us? I wouldn't be much of a match for them, hobbling around on one foot.

There was my M16. The sergeant had brought it back with him. I leaned over, picked it up and cradled it in my arms.

They knew where we were. What if the grenade had been thrown back at us? What if it really was "In-coming," and not just dropped by that idiot? He must have seen something . . . You don't just throw grenades for no reason, not during night ambush.

I checked the M16 to make sure it was still loaded. It felt like a toy made of plastic. Would it work when I needed it? When was the last time I'd cleaned it? It had misfired before. Would it do that to me again? It was a piece of shit.

Why couldn't they give us something substantial to kill people with; something that felt heavy when you picked it up; something that made you feel comfortable and secure.

The gooks had AK47s made of wood. They were heavy. They weren't toys. They were weapons.

The picture became clear. The gooks would come in. I'd be hobbling around, a pathetic cripple on one foot, trying to stay alive, and the M16 wouldn't work.

I would die here . . . tonight . . . just when I thought it was over.

Wouldn't that be just like it always happened? Wouldn't that be typical of this place? Wouldn't that be just like Vietnam?

Suddenly there was a sound in the brush behind me. Still sitting, I spun around and pointed the M16. I heard it again. Whatever it was, it was big. I couldn't see anything. It moved again. The crackling of twigs told me it was coming closer. I felt my heart sink and time suddenly stood still . . .

"Its just a fuckin' lizard."

The black sergeant's words startled me.

"What?" I asked in a low voice as I glanced over at him.

"A lizard. Just a fuckin' lizard!" he repeated, shaking his head at how dumb I was.

Then he turned over and went back to sleep.

What made him so sure it was just a lizard? How could he just go back to sleep?

Maybe he was right. The lizards in Vietnam were three feet long and weighed seven or eight pounds. They looked like miniature dinosaurs and they were all over the place. It was hard to believe that the gooks actually ate the disgusting things.

The night dragged on as I sat there cradling the M16 and jumping at every sound. It wasn't unusual. There had been other nights like this, endless nights spent waiting for the sun.

Whatever the medic had given me was wearing off and the foot began to throb again. I grit my teeth and rocked slowly with the pain.

An eternity passed. Finally the horizon turned a beautiful shade of light pink, telling me I was going to survive. And I could see it now in the dim light . . . a big, ugly, ridiculous lizard. The sleeping bodies around me began to stir as another night passed, bringing us all one day closer to home.

I noticed a guy with his left side bandaged. He'd been on my right when the grenade exploded and had caught some shrapnel. They told him to sit next to me to wait for the dust-off. We sat there in silence, watching the rest of the squad gather their stuff.

Thirty minutes later, everyone was ready to move out and the rest of Charlie Company was moving down the trail toward our position.

When he got to where the two of us were sitting, the Captain stopped and looked down at us. He wasn't happy. He turned his head toward the rest of the company.

"Maybe I should just take all of this dangerous stuff away from you girls so you don't hurt yourselves!" he said to them. Then he looked back at us in disgust and saw my foot.

"It's not that bad," he said. "I had one like that once. You'll be back."

The medivac helicopter appeared overhead as the captain walked away.

The rest of the company walked past and looked down at us. We were getting out of the field, at least for a little while, and they were admiring our wounds like nineteen-year-olds would admire a brand new Corvette.

"Hit in the foot?" one asked as he walked by.

"Yeah."

"That's great man! You'll be out for a while."

"Thanks." I said.

I stuck the foot out so they could see it better — the perfect wound.

The procession continued. Hunched forward under the weight of their rucksacks, they each looked like Christ carrying his cross to Calvary.

They flashed thumbs up signs and peace signs at us as they passed.

"All right, man! Way to go!"

"Number One!"

There was envy on their faces and I felt sorry for them. Maybe they would be lucky enough to get wounded too. At least there was always that hope.

The chopper set down. We hobbled over to it and climbed inside just before it lifted. It banked to the left and Charlie Company disappeared, as though they had never existed.

I stared down at the bloody foot. It was aching again. "The perfect wound," I reminded myself. I suddenly felt light-headed and sick to my stomach.

"This can't really be happening," I thought as the cockpit grew dark. "This has to be a nightmare. How could I possibly have ended up in Vietnam? . . ."

Chapter Three

"The Color Green"

Janie and I were good kids from Catholic families. We met at Seton Hall when she was a Junior and I was in my Senior year.

With graduation, my student deferment ended. I wanted to marry Janie and start a career, but I was sure to be drafted. At least I thought so.

My draft eligibility had been changed from "S2" to "A1," and it was hard to get a job when it was almost certain you wouldn't be around very long.

Since I had a degree, it was possible to be an officer. Maybe if I signed up instead of waiting for my draft notice, they would go easier on me.

Wouldn't my resumé look a lot better if it said my military obligation was over and that I'd been an officer? Maybe I could choose what I wanted to do. Maybe as an officer, your wife could live with you.

Vietnam? I'd never go there, not if I signed up and got the opportunity to pick my job.

The war was going to end soon anyway, wasn't it? Wasn't that the very reason President Johnson had intensified the bombing, so the war would end before I had to go?

I looked down the long, empty hallway lined with the offices of the recruiters. It was the most deserted hallway in the world in 1967.

The doors were open and a recruiting poster stood outside of each office. In the profound silence, the posters seemed to shout out at me as I walked past them, like boardwalk barkers at Point Pleasant.

"We're still looking for a few good men!" the Marine Corps shouted.

"Keep looking," I whispered back.

"Fly Navy!" said the next poster.

"Yeah, that might happen," I responded sarcastically.

"U.S. Coast Guard perhaps?" the third poster asked politely. They obviously had a self-image problem.

The Air Force didn't say much.

"O.K. So you probably won't be a pilot, but maybe we can find something else for you to do . . ."

"No thanks," I said.

The Army poster had no delusions of grandeur. It was realistic. It had resigned itself to the situation. It knew why I was there.

"We just like the color green," it said. "Come on in and we'll get it over with."

"Take a seat," the sergeant said as he stood to shake my hand. "I'm Sergeant Thomas. What can I do for you?"

He looked sharp in his uniform: stripes down the sleeve; medals on his crisp, starched shirt; his hair cut incredibly short.

He sat down behind his desk and leaned forward a bit. He was in his late 20s. The military haircut gave him a no-nonsense, clean look that said, "My country, right or wrong."

This guy was no "Hippie" like the ones I'd seen on television with their shoulder-length, filthy hair, protesting the war, safely protected from the draft by their college deferments.

He was an "American" in the pure, "John Wayne" sense of the word. It was refreshing to look at him.

The country wasn't going to hell after all. Patriots like Sergeant Thomas still existed. They knew what was right and what was wrong. They would see to it that good triumphed over evil. They knew the true meaning of "Mom and apple pie." It wasn't just a phrase or a slogan for them. For them, it was a doctrine . . . one worth dying for.

I sat in the straight-backed, wooden chair closest to the sergeant's desk.

I was dressed in a sportcoat and tie. I thought it made me look educated, but it was warm and uncomfortable, and the sun shining through the window was in my eyes.

"I'm Don Yost," I said. "I'll be graduating from Seton Hall University in June."

As there was absolutely no reaction from the sergeant, I tried to fill the silence and continued.

"I'll have a degree in English Literature and —"

"Did you say English?" he interrupted.

"That's right, English Literature."

"That's Liberal . . . something, isn't it?" he asked.

He was struggling.

"Arts, Liberal Arts," I said, to help him so he wouldn't be embarrassed. "Sometimes they call it Pre-Law."

"Right, Liberal Arts. So, how can I help you."

"Well, with a degree, I understand I can be an officer. Since my college deferment is over, I thought if I sign up I can pick my job instead of waiting to be drafted."

It was like throwing raw meat to a starving lion.

Sergeant Thomas suddenly came alive. His eyes widened and his mouth snapped open like a big fish getting ready to devour a smaller one.

"No problem! No problem at all!"

He could hardly speak. This was going to be easier than I'd thought. He quickly pushed his chair away from the desk, stood up, walked to a file cabinet and tried to open the top drawer. The drawer stuck. He mumbled something under his breath and pounded the top of the cabinet once, then twice, with his fist.

The cabinet finally surrendered and allowed its drawer to be opened with a shrill screech. Whatever he was looking for wasn't needed very often.

"I must really be special," I thought.

The sergeant found what he wanted and returned to the desk, leaving the drawer open.

One folder in the drawer stood above the others. It had the letters "O.C.S." scribbled on it in blue pen.

"Take a look at this," he said, and handed me a brochure. Then he sat down and leaned back in his chair confidently.

I looked at the cover of the brochure. The words "U.S. Army Adjutant General Corps" were printed above what seemed to be my picture. There was a huge, gold American eagle on the front of his hat with a gold braid beneath it. The cuffs of his jacket and the legs of his pants had black, wide officer stripes on them. The insignia on each lapel were red, white and blue American flags.

Instead of tacky sergeant stripes, he wore a gold bar on each epaulet. He carried a briefcase instead of a rifle, and — he was smiling.

A chill ran up my spine. This was better than I'd dared imagine. It was worth going to college, after all. Now it was going to pay off.

"Just wait till Janie sees this!" I thought.

I contained myself so sergeant Thomas wouldn't see my reaction, but when I looked up from the brochure, he had a broad smile on his face.

"What's the Adjutant General Corps?" I asked.

The sergeant then spoke those immortal words for which I will always remember him.

"With your background, I can set you up with a desk job in Germany."

I didn't fully appreciate that the operative words in the sentence were: "set you up."

"You'll start as a Second Lieutenant and come out in three years a Captain."

I made him repeat it.

"Did you say a desk job in Germany?"

"That's right, Germany."

"If I'm married, can my wife live there with me?"

"Absolutely! We provide housing for officers and their ladies," he said. "Sergeants' wives are called 'wives,' but officers' wives are called 'ladies.' "

"An Officer and His Lady." It was like a line from *Gone with the Wind.*

I don't know why he needed to tell me that sergeants' wives were merely "wives." Maybe he was bitter, but he seemed incredibly benevolent about the situation.

Didn't he realize that I was going to be his boss? He would have to obey my commands without question. If we passed on the street, he would have to salute me. He would have to call me "Sir"!

But I would go easy on him. I would be a good boss, "an officer and a gentleman." I would at least see to it that he got a submissive file cabinet, one that wouldn't object to having its drawers opened.

My daydream ended when the sergeant slammed his desk drawer and started searching among the papers on his desk for a pen. As he searched, he recited lines like a kid in a school play.

"You'll start out at Fort Dix for Basic and Advanced training. You won't have to start until September. After that, you'll go to Officer Candidate School in Fort Benning, Georgia . . .

"Where did that pen go?

"That's a six-month course. It's not easy, but you won't have any problem. It's Infantry training, but that's only a formality. Everybody goes through Infantry training . . .

"Oh, here it is!"

He found his pen on the floor.

"Slow down a minute," I said. "What do you mean by a 'formality'?"

He disappeared as he leaned over to pick up his pen. His muffled voice came back from under the desk.

"Like I said, it's a formality. Everybody goes through Infantry training in the Army, just like West Point. That's all Infantry. It's how we train officers. It doesn't mean you'll be in the Infantry."

When he reappeared he was smiling; to reassure me, I thought, but more likely because he'd found his pen.

How could I have been be so foolish as to question him? Of course it made sense . . . "Just like West Point." How else would the Army train its officers? Officer Candidate School would be just like West Point.

The sergeant was waiting for my answer.

"It sounds good. I'll get back to you," I said as I stood to shake his hand.

"You'll have to decide soon. Within the next week if you want to start in September."

"Thank you," I said.

The sergeants' file cabinet gave a final screech as he slammed its drawer shut. I stepped out of the office and into the deserted hallway.

The recruiting posters were silent now as I quickly walked past them. I'd made up my mind. Sergeant Thomas had said the words

I'd hoped to hear. I was going to be an officer. Janie and I could get married. I'd have a job to support us and we would be together in Germany. It was all going to come true.

Janie would be an Officer's lady . . . my lady. She was intelligent and she was beautiful and I was proud of her.

I imagined us arriving at a military ball. I would be wearing my dress blue officer's uniform with its dark blue jacket and gold-trimmed epaulets as I escorted her into the ballroom. She would be gorgeous in a white evening gown with a modest neckline, trimmed in sequins. The moonlight would reflect the golden highlights of her light brown hair which would be swept up, accenting the delicate features of her pretty face.

Her soft brown eyes would sparkle as they always did and everyone would notice her as we waited to be announced. A hush would fill the room, followed by envious whispers, as we paused at the top of the stairway.

"Lieutenant and Mrs. Yost," they would say. Janie would look at me and smile as I offered her my arm and we would slowly descend the staircase of the room she had captivated.

I couldn't wait to tell her the good news. . . .

Chapter Four

"Building the Cross"

"I went to see the Army Recruiter today," I told her as we sat in her mother's living room. "I can be an officer in Germany. They have housing there for officers and their wives."

Janie didn't say anything. She seemed stunned. I fumbled through my pockets for the brochure, but I couldn't find it. I must have left it on the sergeant's desk.

"I don't have to go until September. After six months of Officer Candidate School — that's like West Point — I'll be a Lieutenant and we can live in Germany."

I thought "West Point" would get her attention, but there was no response. I fumbled again for the brochure, the one with my picture on it, the magical brochure that would make her proud of me.

"I'll have to go to Basic and Advanced training before that, but that's at Fort Dix. It's not that far away. Then I have to go to Fort Benning for O.C.S. That's in Georgia."

Something was being lost in the translation. Maybe I wasn't explaining it right. Where was sergeant Thomas when you needed him? I was getting desperate.

"Sergeants' wives are called "Wives" but officers' wives are called "Ladies.""

She looked as if she wanted to cry. I thought maybe she was upset about what would be expected of her.

"You might have to go to an occasional party . . . It's important for an officer and his lady to be sociable . . . I guess we would have to go."

There was hurt in her voice when she spoke.

"Why are you doing this? . . ."

It was hard to believe that one question could wipe away all the excitement I felt when I left the recruiter's office, but it did.

The Cinderella fairy tale in my head made me feel foolish now.

"You won't be there for my graduation," she said.

I suddenly knew that I had let her down. How could I not realize that I would miss her graduation? It hadn't even occurred to me. I never even told her that I was going to talk to the recruiter. I should've told her.

I was embarrassed by how thoughtless I'd been, but like a school kid bringing home a bad report card, I got defensive.

"What else am I supposed to do, wait to get drafted? How am I going to get a job if they know I'm A1?"

"Dinner's ready," her mother called from the kitchen.

Janie got up and walked out of the room. I stayed behind trying to figure out what had happened. This was not going well. Why couldn't she understand that I didn't have a choice? Why didn't she realize that I was doing this for her, so that we could get married and so I could take care of her?

How could we get married if I didn't have a job? Even if I found someone stupid enough to hire me, how long would it last before I got my draft notice? Janie would have to go back to live with her parents and I would have to go to Vietnam.

There was no question in my mind that that was exactly what would happen. People were burning their draft cards and running to Canada to avoid the draft, but that just wasn't me. I wasn't going to be a draft dodger and maybe even end up in jail. That was for the spoiled "intellectuals" from Berkeley, not for a good kid who put himself through Seton Hall by working full time at the post office.

I remembered the brochure with my picture on it. The solution seemed so obvious. . . .

When I walked into the kitchen, Janie's mother was serving dinner. She had made Polish meatballs and mashed potatoes and it smelled delicious. I pulled a chair from the table and sat down across from Janie. The atmosphere was tense as we sat there without speaking.

"What's the matter?" her mother finally asked.

"He's going to join the Army," Janie told her.

There was bitterness in her voice.

She could have said "Don's going to join the Army," but saying "He" made me feel like they were talking *about* me, as if I wasn't even in the room.

"Why?" her mother asked.

"I don't know. Why don't you ask him?"

"This is just great," I thought. How was I supposed to explain all the reasons?

I wanted to say, "Because I love your daughter."

I wanted to say, "I'm doing it for Janie so that I'll have a job and we can get married."

I wanted to say, "So that I can be an Officer and she'll be proud of me."

I wanted to say, "Because I have an obligation to my country."

I wanted to say, "Because I'm no draftcard-burning hippie."

Instead, I said, "Because I'm going to get drafted anyway . . ."

"You don't know that," Janie said.

She was right. I didn't know for certain.

"Is it because your father was in the Army? Are you trying to impress him? Is that why?"

My father? What did he have to do with this?

"You don't have to join the Army just because your father had to go," her mother said.

"It's not because of my father. He doesn't have anything to do with this."

I wasn't anything like my father. He drank and he was loud. You knew when he walked into a room. He was always yelling at my mother and I felt sorry for her. They had an understanding between them that he was the boss, the head of the family. But my mother kept it together and somehow you knew that he couldn't make it without her.

My mother told me once that he was a skinny kid who got picked on when he was growing up and that he wasn't always like this; not until after the war.

"He was different when he came home," she told me.

But it didn't make any difference. She would stay with him, "for better or worse." Catholics didn't get divorced, "No matter what." And she loved him.

I understood, somehow. At least I thought I did, as much as a kid is able to understand why his father drinks. I needed to understand or try to. I was the oldest of nine kids. I had a responsibility to make some sense of it.

I understood that Catholics weren't allowed to use birth-control. My mother had gone to the priest and asked him for permission, but Father Reilley told her that if she practiced birth-control, she would go to Hell. There was no doubt. There was no question. But most of all, there was no compassion.

It would be her "cross" in life to raise nine kids and they had better be "good" ones. It didn't matter that her husband drank. That was just part of her cross, its crossbar. She had no choice.

I often wondered how Father Reilley would like being in Hell. There was no question in my mind that there was a special place reserved for him there.

I remembered spending hours in the car waiting for my father outside the American Legion while he was getting loaded. He'd sit at the bar and turn the foot of his artificial leg around backwards waiting for people to be shocked by it. He thought it was funny. I didn't.

He told the story about the doctor examining his leg in the hospital. The doctor said it was bad. Maybe he could try to save it with pins and wires, but it probably wouldn't work. The doctor pulled back the blanket and my father sat up to look at it. It was only hanging by a thread.

"I looked the doctor straight in the eye," he said, "and told him 'cut it off.' "

The doctor was used to dealing with whimpering "Crybabies" and had finally found a "Good soldier." He smiled and put his hand on my father's shoulder.

"You're going to be just fine son," he told him.

"Good soldiers" never cried in World War II. They were "men." They were "heroes." They willingly did what they had to do for their country, no matter what the sacrifice. They had gotten rid of Adolf Hitler and had bombed Hiroshima back to the stone age and God was grateful. My mother told me once that they said when an American soldier was killed in World War II, he fell into the arms of our Blessed Mother.

No, "good soldiers" never cried in World War II. If what happened to them or what they did to other people ever bothered them, they never told anyone. "Heroes" didn't complain. They just joined the American Legion where they could get cheap booze and become alcoholics; where they could try to bury their hurt and anger, close the wound, hide the scar.

Their families, the ones who loved them, would have to deal with it. It would become their problem. They would wait in cars outside American Legion Posts and spend hours worrying if Dad would be coming home drunk again. They would spend Christmas picking up the broken ornaments after he had fallen into the tree.

They would make calls to the local bars asking if their father was there, only to hear him in the background telling the bartender to lie for him.

They would make the excuses for him: "You'll have to excuse my father; he was in the war you know." Their hearts would be torn between loving him and hating him. And they would watch their mother as she cried.

I hated the American Legion . . .

"This has nothing to do with my father," I told them again. "I just need to get this over with."

"But what if you have to go to Vietnam?" Janie asked.

"I won't. The Sergeant told me that most people don't go there. We'd be able to live in Germany and I'll be an officer. He told me that. I wish I'd remembered that brochure he showed me."

"It's only for three years," I continued. "If I wait to get drafted I'll be in for two anyway."

Janie's father hadn't been in the service. Maybe she and her mother didn't understand that there were other things you could do besides be in the Infantry. I thought it would help if I explained it.

"See, I won't be in the Infantry. The Infantry is the bad part, where all the shooting is. If I just wanted to impress my father, I'd join the Infantry. That's what he was in. He told me once, "Whatever you do, stay out of the Infantry." I could end up in that if I got drafted."

He really did tell me to "Stay out of the infantry." He had been drinking and was lost in deep thought when he'd said it. It was a sentence from nowhere. He was staring down at the table and mumbled it half to himself as I passed by.

I finished trying to "hard sell" Janie and her mother on the idea of my joining the Army. There was nothing I could say that would make them happy about it. Janie wasn't going to enjoy this burden that was being forced upon her. She didn't like the fact that I was going to miss her graduation and she didn't want to be "An Officer's lady" and have to live in Germany. She wouldn't be proud of me in my officer's uniform. It was green. She hated the color green and she thought I was doing this to impress my father.

My fairy tale daydream had become a nightmare, an ordeal to be lived through. But I couldn't see any other way. I thought Janie would come around eventually. She'd understand that I was doing this for her. It would all work out somehow. She'd be proud of me in my officer's uniform, even if it was green. She might even like living in Germany.

I waited a day or two to think things over. Then I went back to the recruiter's office and signed the papers. I had no way of knowing that I had begun building a cross that Janie and I would share for years to come . . .

Chapter Five

"Ultimate Weapon"

The summer of 1967 passed quickly. September came and I reported to the Post Office in Paterson to be sworn in.

It was an old, musty building. Its wooden floor creaked and its wire-meshed windows allowed only a little light to shine through. I felt like a kid on the first day of school as I walked into room #314.

A black sergeant stood behind a desk. He had the face of a bulldog. Wooden chairs had been set in rows facing him. I took a seat near the back and watched the other guys as they drifted in.

We were an unlikely group, black, white, brown and yellow, all different shapes and sizes, and all there for the same reason. We sat there in silence like strangers in an elevator on its way down; staring at the numbers; each lost in his own thoughts. Thirty minutes passed before the bulldog barked.

"Aw-rite! . . . Listen Up!"

I'd never heard anyone say "Listen-up" before. I didn't understand why he needed to say "Up."

"I am Staff Sergeant Johnson . . . You will call me "Sergeant." When I tell you people to "Fall in," you will form a line up to the desk. You will have your papers with you. I will tell you where to sit. Are there any questions, people?"

He looked around the room to see if there were any questions. There weren't.

"Aw-rite! . . . Fall In!"

As we approached his desk, he found our names on a roster and told us which side of the room to sit on.

"Gonzales, Enrico, H . . . right side!"

"Clark, Martin G . . . left side!"

"Aba . . . Abamonte, Francis J . . . left side!"

28

Abamonte was confused and sat down on the right side of the room.

"Yo! . . . I said left side!" the sergeant yelled.

"Your "other" left side!"

A chuckle swept through the room as Abamonte moved across the aisle.

The sergeant continued his litany.

"Peters . . . Paul M . . . right side!"

"Deloro . . . Anthony L . . . left side!"

Next in line was a skinny kid with shoulder-length hair.

"Murphy, Martin J . . . lef' . . ."

He stopped in mid-sentence and stared at him.

"You a 'Flower child,' boy?"

Murphy's face turned bright red.

"N . . . n . . . no Sir." he stammered.

The sergeant's eyes narrowed . . . The muscles of his big, square jaw tightened . . . The veins in his neck were about to burst. He slowly stepped from behind the desk like a rattlesnake coiling itself; preparing to strike.

Murphy took an awkward step backward. The sergeant put his hands on his hips and leaned forward until his face was only a half-inch away from Murphy's.

"DON'T . . . CALL . . . ME . . . SIR!" he bellowed, loud enough to make the windows rattle.

"I WORK FOR A LIVIN'!"

"IS THAT CLEAR, BOY! . . ."

"Y . . . Y . . . Yes." Murphy whimpered.

"YES . . . WHAT! . . ." The sergeant yelled.

"Ye . . . Yes . . . Sergeant."

"I CAN'T HEAR YOU! . . ."

"Y . . . Y . . . Yes Sergeant!" Murphy repeated, louder this time. His hands were shaking. He was going to cry.

Sergeant Johnson finally took his hands from his hips.

"You Are Sorry! . . ." he said, and went back to his desk.

"Murphy . . . Martin, J . . . Left side!"

Murphy wiped his face with his sleeve and took a seat . . . on the right side of the room.

"YOU ARE SORRY, MISTER! . . ." The sergeant yelled.

"I SAID "LEF' SIDE"! . . . YOUR "MILITARY" LEF'
SIDE!"

There was no chuckling this time as Murphy moved to his
"Military" left side of the room.

The procession continued until each of us had been told where
to sit. The guy on my right leaned toward me.

"He should never have come in here with his hair like that," he
said.

"You can say that again. He's going to have a rough time . . .
I'm Don Yost."

"Chuck Pruit," he said as we shook hands.

"Did you get drafted?" I asked him.

"No, I signed up. I'm going to be an officer."

"Me too."

Chuck Pruit didn't look like an officer. He looked like an accountant.

He was pudgy, a Pillsbury Doughboy with glasses.

"Did you go to college?" I asked him.

"Yeah . . . Rutgers."

"Oh, on the banks of the old Raritan?"

"That's right!" Chuck smiled.

"How do you know my school song?" he asked.

"My uncle went to Rutgers. He took me to a couple of their
football games."

"List'n Up!" the sergeant shouted.

"When Captain Miller comes into the room, you will snap to
attention. He will swear you in."

The sergeant sat down behind his desk and began fumbling
with papers. A low murmur filled the room as people began talking
with one another. I glanced across the aisle at Murphy. He wasn't
speaking to anyone. He just sat there on his "Military" left side of
the room staring at his sneakers. I felt sorry for him.

After twenty minutes Captain Miller stepped into the room and
the sergeant jumped to his feet.

"A TIN . . . HUT!"

"What? . . . What did he say? . . ."

"What language was that?" I asked Chuck.

"I have no idea."

"BANG! BANG! BANG!". . . . It sounded like rifle shots as the wooden chairs collapsed and crashed to the floor.

"We people" did our best to "Snap" to Attention, but it was difficult to "Snap" when you were bending down to pick up a chair.

Staff Sergeant Johnson was not impressed.

"LEAVE THEM THERE! . . . JUST LEAVE THE CHAIRS WHERE THEY ARE!"

When quiet finally returned, the Captain marched to the front of the room. He moved like a mechanical duck in a shooting gallery. He didn't look anything like the officer on the cover of the brochure Sergeant Thomas had shown me. He had a huge, long nose . . . a beak.

He returned the sergeant's salute and pivoted to face us. He fixed his eyes on the clock at the back of the room and began to recite lines in a high pitched squeaky voice . . . a quack.

"Raise your right hand and repeat after me."

"I (State your name) solemnly swear . . ."

"I (State your name) solemnly swear," half of us repeated.

"No! I mean *say* your name . . . your own name!" he quacked.

We got through it . . . somehow.

"Welcome to the United States Army," he said dryly.

He pivoted again, returned the sergeant's salute and marched out of the room.

The swearing in "Ceremony" couldn't have taken more than a minute and a half. We had been told to report "promptly" at 1:00. I glanced at the clock on the wall. It was now 4:30 . . . it seemed later.

Another thirty-minute eternity passed before Sergeant Johnson finally stepped from behind his desk.

"Aw-rite! . . . List'n Up!"

"You will fall in on the right side of the room. You will move out to the diner across the street for chow. You will have ten minutes to eat. FALL IN!"

More chairs crashed as we "Fell in" on the right side of the room.

"A . . . TIN . . . HUT!"

We came to attention.

"LEF' . . . FACE!"

We turned to the left . . . most of us did.

"FORWARD . . . MARCH!"

We followed Sergeant Johnson through the door, down the hall, and out of the building like school kids following their teacher on a field trip to the post office.

Chuck Pruit was on line in front of me and I spoke to the back of his head.

"See Chuck, he's not so bad. . . . He's taking us to dinner. He even made reservations."

He glanced back at me.

"I didn't have anything to eat all day," he said. "Maybe I'll have a couple of Texas wieners and some fries."

Sergeant Johnson opened the door to the "P.O. Dinner" and we followed him inside. A waitress said something to him and led us to a back room. She wanted to keep us "away from the regular customers."

The room had a sour smell to it. It was barely lit by a single light bulb hanging from the ceiling by an extension cord. There were no windows and the grey paint was peeling from the walls. Wooden folding tables and chairs were set in rows. Chuck had wasted his time trying to decide what he was going to eat. The decision had been made for us. It was already waiting on plates. It had been waiting a long time.

"Aw-rite, you've got ten minutes!" Sergeant Johnson reminded us.

We pulled our chairs from the table and sat down. The sergeant stood at one end of the room with his arms folded and looked at his wristwatch. He wouldn't be joining us. I took one look at what was on my plate and understood why he wasn't eating.

It must have been chicken long ago, but now it was hard to be sure. It had a sweet, rotting smell to it. Next to it was a spoonful of what might have been peas at one time. I picked up the red, plastic tumbler next to the plate and took a sip of whatever was in it. It was water. Chuck was sitting across from me. I watched him as he slowly put a piece of whatever the meat was into his mouth. He immediately gagged and covered his mouth with a napkin. Sergeant Johnson was suddenly standing behind him.

"You got a problem, boy?" he asked in a tone that told Chuck that he had better not have a problem.

"N . . . No sergeant!" Chuck answered.

I thought I would risk it and try the peas.

"What can they do to ruin peas?" I wondered.

I was about to touch one of them with my fork when it moved.

"This garbage should have been thrown out a week ago," I thought.

I couldn't eat it. No matter what the sergeant might do to me. I envisioned what the invoice would say when it was presented for payment: "26 Chicken Dinners, with Beverage. . . . $867."

I wondered how much of a kickback the sergeant was getting. "He's got to be making a fortune on this," I thought.

"Aw-rite! You're done!" he barked after a few moments.

He must have known that none of us would need the entire ten minutes.

He marched us out of the back room, past the "regular customers" and outside to a yellow school bus waiting at the curb. We filed past him as we boarded the bus that would take us down the New Jersey Turnpike to Fort Dix. The sergeant wouldn't be going with us and that was good.

After two hours, I realized that Fort Dix was much farther from Clifton – and Janie – than I'd imagined. Another thirty minutes passed before we saw the sign that read "Fort Dix . . . Maguire Airforce Base . . . Next Exit."

"We're almost in Pennsylvania!" someone said. Pennsylvania? Pennsylvania was far; really far. I was beginning to feel lonely.

Everyone was silent as the bus lumbered down the exit ramp. A few minutes later we arrived at the main gate and there it was: a statue of an infantry soldier in combat.

He looked the way my uncle Frank must have looked just before he was killed. It was the picture of him that I'd carried in my mind from the time I was a little kid.

He was a paratrooper in World War II.

"A hero," they said, "killed trying to save a buddy."

His name was engraved on the war memorial in Totowa. I used to stop and look at it on my way home from grammar school, trying to imagine what he was like. I never knew him, but I had seen pictures of him in his uniform. He was smiling and had his foot on the bumper of an old Buick. He was handsome.

I remembered when they brought his closed casket home and set it in my grandmother's livingroom.

"His brains were in his helmet," someone had told her. "He never knew what hit him."

Beneath the statue of my uncle Frank were the words that I had no way of knowing, foretold my future.

"Welcome to Fort Dix," they said, "Home of the Ultimate Weapon."

Chapter Six

"The Apparition"

Its brakes squealed as the bus came to a stop. The door opened and an apparition from Hell materialized in the aisle before us. It took the form of a sergeant.

He wore a brown "Smokey-the-Bear" hat with a shiny, brass eagle on the band. It was pulled down low in front so that it touched his eyebrows.

Red, blood-shot eyes looked out at us from under its wide brim like a lizard peering out from under its rock. His hair was cut so short that the sides of his head were white. The shirt of his tan uniform was stiff with starch. Above one pocket was his name tag: "Decker." His pants were bloused above his spit-shined boots and his hands were on his hips. The expression on his square-jawed face said he was angry about something . . . maybe we were late. He pointed at Murphy.

"WHAT'S THAT GIRL DOING ON MY BUS!"

He spit the words at us in a thick, southern drawl.

It was a rhetorical question . . . none of us answered him.

"ARE YOU QUEER, BOY? . . . ARE THEY SENDING ME QUEERS NOW?!"

Murphy didn't say anything.

"Damn Flower Child . . ." Decker mumbled to himself.

The blood-shot eyes looked us over, sizing us up like we were sides of beef hanging from meat hooks in a slaughterhouse.

He shook his head. He was disgusted as if he'd been stuck with a load of rotting meat . . . again.

"YOU PEOPLE ARE SORRY!" he shouted. "AT MY COM-MAND YOU WILL GET YOUR SORRY ASSES OFF OF MY BUS!"

We hadn't realized that Decker owned the bus, that it was his personal property, that we were trespassing.

"If I knew it was your bus, I'd have found another way to get here," I thought as he glared at me. It felt good to yell back at him from the safety of my thoughts.

"DO YOU UNDERSTAND ME, PEOPLE?"

"Yes," we responded with one voice.

"YES . . . WHAT!"

"Yes, Sergeant."

"I CAN'T . . . HEAR . . . YOU!"

He chanted the words, raising his voice to a high pitch at the word "hear" and then dropping to a lower pitch at the word "you."

"Yes, Sergeant!" we yelled back as loud as we could.

"MOVE OUT!"

We crammed into the narrow aisle, bumping into each other. He stood by the door and yelled.

"MOVE! . . . MOVE! . . . MOVE!"

Outside, three more sergeants yelled at us to stand on white footprints that were painted on the asphalt.

We felt ridiculous in our jeans and sport shirts. We didn't belong; worthless as clowns at a funeral. We were "sorry."

"A . . . TIN . . . N . . . N . . . N . . . HUT!" Decker shouted.

"AT MY COMMAND YOU WILL ASSUME THE PUSH-UP POSITION . . . YOU DO KNOW WHAT THE PUSH-UP POSITION IS, DON'T YOU?"

"Yes . . . Sergeant!"

"DROP!"

The rough asphalt dug deep into the palms of our hands as we dropped.

We would be there for a while – an eternity, while the sergeants stood over us watching, not saying anything, waiting for us to feel the strain.

An endless two minutes dragged by. We were feeling it now . . .

Our arms began shaking . . .

Our backs ached . . .

The asphalt dug deeper into our palms . . .

"I can't last much longer . . ." I thought,

"Not . . . much . . . longer . . ."

Another eternity passed.

The muscles between my shoulder blades ached. They had turned to knots and the rope was being drawn tighter. Salty sweat stung my eyes making the asphalt blur . . .

"I'm . . . not . . . going . . . to . . . make it . . . God, it hurts."

I glanced at the guy on my right. His back was arched like a cat to relieve the pressure but his arms were still shaking.

"YOU EYE-BALLIN' ME, BOY?!" Decker shouted.

Chuck had made the fatal mistake of looking up at him.

"N . . . No Sergeant."

His voice sounded pathetic.

"GIVE ME TWENTY!"

Chuck started doing push-ups.

"COUNT THEM OFF! BY THE NUMBERS!"

"One . . . . two . . . ."

"ONE . . . WHAT?!"

"One . . . Sergeant."

"I CAN'T HEAR YOU!"

"One Sergeant! . . . . .two Sergeant . . ."

There was no way he was going to be able to do it.

He was overweight. It was a miracle that he was still able to hold the position, never mind do the exercise.

The sergeants prowled among us like lions stalking their prey.

"STRAIGHTEN YOUR BACK!" one yelled at Murphy.

The only response was an anguished moan.

"STRAIGHTEN UP, TRAINEE!" The sergeant yelled again.

"I . . . can't do it, Sergeant . . . ."

"YOU CAN'T DO IT! . . . YOU CAN'T DO IT! . . . IS SOMETHIN' THE MATTER WITH YOU, BOY?! . . . WAS YOUR MOTHER ON DRUGS WHEN SHE HAD YOU?! . . . YOU GOT SOME KIND OF DRUG PROBLEM BOY . . . ?!"

"No . . . Sergeant."

Another lion roared at Murphy.

"GET UP OFF YOUR KNEES, PRINCESS!"

"STRAIGHTEN UP!"

"YOU MISSIN' MOMMA . . . BOY?"

"No, Sergeant," Murphy said.

"Three . . . . sergeant . . . . .fou . . . .four . . ."

Chuck's pushups were slowing down. I remembered him saying that he hadn't had anything to eat all day. The mouthful of spoiled chicken wasn't helping him now.

"I AM DRILL SERGEANT DECKER!" Decker yelled.

"No . . . kidding," I thought. (I couldn't keep my arms from shaking.)

"YOU WILL CALL ME *SERGEANT!*"

"That's different . . ." (My wrists were throbbing.)

"YOU PEOPLE ARE SORRY!"

"Oh . . . Really? . . ." (My toes had gone numb.)

"GIVE YOUR SOUL TO GOD AND YOUR HEART TO MOMMA . . . YOUR ASS IS MINE!"

"Did you write that . . . all by yourself?" (I arched my back.)

"DO YOU UNDERSTAND ME PEOPLE?"

"Yes . . . Sergeant!" we yelled at the asphalt.

"I CAN'T HEAR YOU!"

"Yes . . . Sergeant!"

There was a bitter sound to our voices. We were hurting . . . we were frustrated . . . we were angry . . . what was the point of treating us like this?

"Four . . . . ser . . . geant . . . ."

He wasn't going to make it. Chuck was trying, really trying to push the asphalt away from him, but nothing was happening. He may as well have been trying to push the entire planet out of its orbit.

"ARE YOU DYING ON MY ASPHALT . . . TRAINEE?"

"N . . . no, Sergeant," he whimpered.

He could barely speak. The sweat was pouring down his face. His glasses had fogged. He was about to collapse.

"DID I ORDER YOU TO DIE ON MY ASPHALT, TRAINEE?"

"No . . . Sergeant."

"YOU WILL DIE AT MY COMMAND . . . AND ONLY AT MY COMMAND!"

"Die at his command? This guy is sick!" I thought.

"IS THAT UNDERSTOOD?"

"Yes . . . Sergeant."

"A TIN . . . N . . . N . . . HUT!"

Finally! We groaned and came to attention. My legs and arms were stiff. I looked at my hands. They were red. The asphalt had left its imprint on them.

"HANDS AT YOUR SIDES! . . . HEELS TOGETHER! . . . EYES FRONT!"

The lions were still hunting. One of them attacked.

Its face was suddenly half an inch away from mine.

"HEELS TOGETHER! . . . EYES FRONT!" it roared.

I felt its warm spit hit my face as I tried to keep my eyes to the front. He must have been drinking the night before, I could smell the stale liquor on his hot breath.

Decker kept us there at attention while his lions mauled us. He was letting them have some fun. It must have been a few days since they'd last tasted raw meat.

He was enjoying the spectacle . . . a Roman Emperor watching his pets devour Christians.

He grew tired of the sport, eventually.

"LEFT . . . FACE!"

We turned to the left . . . most of us did.

"DOUBLE-TIME . . . MARCH!"

Our legs were sore now. It was an effort to move them. Decker ran in front of us. We followed not knowing where we were going. The lions ran along side, ready to attack any of us of who were too weak or too "sorry" to keep up. We approached one of the white, wooden buildings.

"COMPANY . . . HALT!"

"PARADE . . . REST!"

We did our best to imitate the sergeants with their feet apart and their hands locked behind their backs. Decker disappeared inside the building. We waited for him . . . and waited for him. He finally re-appeared.

"A . . . TIN . . . HUT!"

"FORWARD . . . MARCH!"

We filed into the building. It had the moth-ball smell of a dry goods store. There were long tables with piles of drab, green clothing on them. We would finally be able to get rid of our civilian clothes.

Behind the tables stood Privates who shoved our stuff at us as we filed past.

"Move!" the first one yelled, and shoved a fistfull of ugly green underwear into my stomach.

"Who the hell are you?" I thought.

I didn't see any stripes on his sleeve . . . a loser on a power trip.

I read the label on the underwear. It was written in a strange language. It looked like English, but all the words were . . . backwards.

"Shorts . . . Boxer . . . Mens . . . Olive Green."

The next guy shoved ugly, green shirts at me.

"Jacket . . . Fatigue . . . Mens . . . Olive Green."

"Keep it movin', Trainee!"

The third guy piled ugly, green pants on top of the ugly underwear and ugly shirts.

"Trousers . . . Fatigue . . . Mens . . . Olive Green."

"Move it! . . . Move it!" he yelled.

They all seemed to have the same bitter attitude. I would learn that it was affectionately referred to as: "A Case of the Ass."

It got its name from the assumption that everybody in the Army must have hemorrhoids . . . that's what made them irritable. It should have had a label like the ugly, green underwear:

"Attitude . . . Ass . . . Case of the . . . Olive Green . . . One Each."

When we got outside, our arms were full, piled high with: "Clothing . . . Army . . . Mens . . . (You will come to hate) . . . Olive Green."

Chapter Seven

"Sacred Soil"

"How are you doing?" I asked Chuck.

"I don't feel so good," he said.

"I think I'm gonna throw up."

He didn't look good either. His face was paste white.

"You shouldn't have eaten that chicken." I told him.

"Chicken? . . . Is that what it was?"

"A . . . TIN . . . HUT!" It was Decker's voice.

We tried to come to attention with clothes piled to our chins.

"AT MY COMMAND, YOU WILL MARCH DOUBLE-TIME TO THE BARRACKS."

"YOU WILL HAVE EXACTLY THREE MINUTES TO GET RID OF YOUR SORRY CIVILIAN CLOTHES."

"YOU WILL FALL-IN OUTSIDE THE BARRACKS, DRESSED IN COMBAT BOOTS, FATIGUE PANTS AND T-SHIRTS."

"LEFT . . . FACE!"

We turned to the left . . . most of us did.

"FORWARD . . . MARCH!"

The barracks were one-story, wooden, white buildings with shingle roofs. They stood at attention in neat rows. They were all exactly the same except for the black numbers above each door.

We ran through the open door of building 21B. Inside were metal bunk beds with wooden foot lockers. It looked like a hospital ward. Apparently all the patients had died the night before. The bodies had been disposed of and the thin mattresses of their beds had been rolled up, exposing the springs. A brown, woolen blanket was folded neatly on top of each mattress.

"I have to go to the bathroom." Chuck said.

He dropped his arm full of clothes and ran to the far end of the barracks to a door marked "Latrine."

It was complete insanity as the rest of us ran to a bed, threw our stuff down on it and started changing clothes.

When Chuck got back he looked a little better.

"We only have another minute!" someone yelled.

"You won't believe it!" Chuck said as he threw his stuff on the bunk above mine and tore off his civilian clothes.

"There aren't any partitions in there! Just eight toilets in a row . . . you have to sit there . . . in front of everybody!"

Clothing was being thrown in every direction. A moment later we were standing outside the barracks in our fatigues.

"A . . . TIN . . . HUT!" Decker yelled and started taking roll call.

"BAKER! . . ."

"Here!"

"GONZALES . . ."

"Here!"

"MARTIN! . . ."

"Here!"

"MURPHY! . . ."

There was silence.

"MURPHY! . . ." he yelled a second time.

Still no response.

"Where's Murphy?" I whispered to Chuck from the corner of my mouth.

He didn't have to answer. Murphy was standing in the doorway, frantically trying to stuff his T-shirt into his pants. His shoulder-length hair looked even more ridiculous with a military uniform.

"Here . . . Sergeant," he said meekly.

"DROP!" Decker yelled.

Murphy dropped.

"GIVE ME TWENTY!"

"GIRLS TAKE LONGER TO GET DRESSED!" Decker scoffed as Murphy began doing pushups.

"One . . . Sergeant . . . Two . . . Sergeant . . . Three . . . Sergeant."

Decker finished the roll call just as Murphy struggled through his twentieth push-up and got in line.

We followed Decker to a building that had a sign with the words "Barber Shop" painted on it in red and white letters.

Inside, two civilians stood behind barber chairs waiting for us with their clippers at the ready. Their expressions told us they were bored.

It was the world's quickest haircut. It seemed as though they weren't cutting hair as much as they were shearing sheep. There was no expertise required here, just a pair of electric clippers that they ran from front to back, bottom to top.

"No wonder they're bored," I thought. "How can they do this day in and day out?"

One of the "barbers" seemed to have a perverted sense of humor, stemming from his boredom no doubt. As each guy sat in his chair he would question them, like a real barber would.

"How 'bout if I leave just a little bit on top?" he would ask.

"Sure, that would be good," the sheep would respond.

"BUZZZZZ"

Nothing was left on top.

"Next!"

"What if I leave the sideburns just a little long?"

"That would be great."

"BUZZZZZ"

There were no sideburns.

"Next! . . . Just a trim?"

"Yes, please."

"BUZZZZZ"

To . . . the . . . bone.

"Next!"

Murphy was next. He climbed into the perverted barber's chair. The barber walked around to the front and pushed Murphy's chin first to the right, then to the left studying the shoulder length hair.

He must have been fantasizing about what he could do if only they would let him . . . bangs? . . . a flip? . . . a perm perhaps?

"BUZZZZZ"

The fantasy fell to the floor along with Murphy's personality. Those of us who witnessed it gasped.

The perverted barber wasn't a barber at all! He was't a witchdocter! He had shrunk Murphy's head to half its size and had given him huge, elephant ears! Murphy as we knew him no longer existed.

When it was over, we all had "haircuts" exactly like Decker . . . "White Sidewalls."

We all had ears exactly like Murphy's . . . huge elephant ears.

We had been raped; raped by a perverted witchdoctor.

Decker didn't tell us where we were going next. We found ourselves standing outside a building that had a medicinal smell to it . . . a "Clinic."

He lined us up single-file at the front door and told us to roll up the sleeves of our T-shirts.

"WHEN YOU ARE INSIDE THIS BUILDING, YOU WILL KEEP YOUR EYES TO THE FRONT."

"IS THAT CLEAR?"

"Yes . . . Sergeant."

"WHEN THEY ARE FINISHED GIVING YOU YOUR IN-OCULATIONS, YOU WILL IMMEDIATELY RUN BACK TO THE BARRACKS!"

"YOU WILL NOT WALK . . . YOU WILL RUN!"

"TRAINEES DO NOT WALK!"

"IS THAT UNDERSTOOD?"

"Yes . . . Sergeant."

I was a little nervous about getting shots.

"They must know what they're doing." I thought. "It'll be over quickly . . ."

We weren't ready for what we saw and heard when the door opened. There were two rows of guys in green fatigues. Each was holding what looked like a silver pistol.

"FRESH MEAT! . . . FRESH TRAINEE MEAT!"

They shrieked the words at us like demented banshees. There were shrill rebel yells and loud cat calls. We would have to walk the aisle between them while they injected us with whatever was in the guns. I could barely hear the guy behind me over the screaming.

"Oh, Man! . . . Not those guns!"

"What? . . . What did you say?"

I turned my head toward him. His eyes were wide open with fear. He leaned forward and had to shout so I could hear him.

"THOSE GUNS! . . . IF YOU MOVE WHEN THEY'RE SQUEEZING THE TRIGGER, YOU GET CUT!"

"WHAT IF THEY MOVE?" I yelled back.

He didn't hear me and I didn't need an answer.

The procession of "Fresh Trainee Meat" had started through the gauntlet. The rebel yells and screams were even louder now. It was a scene from Dante's "Inferno."

I was determined to keep my eyes to the front. I would fix them on the back of the head of the guy in front of me. I wouldn't move when they pulled the trigger no matter what.

The screaming grew to a frenzy. The wooden floor was getting sticky . . . sticky with blood . . . "Sorry Trainee blood."

"YOU MOVED, TRAINEE!" He was laughing.

I didn't feel it at first. Then it came . . . a dull ache in my left shoulder. He must have hit bone.

I knew I hadn't moved.

"So this is how it's gonna be." I thought as the second guy cut my right shoulder and yelled at me for moving. Both shoulders were hurting now as if to balance the pain.

The banshees were feasting on us.

The left shoulder was cut again, then the right, then the left.

Somehow, I made it to the end and found myself outside with both arms throbbing. I looked at my shoulders, there were streams of blood running down both arms. It dripped from my elbows and disappeared into the sacred soil of Fort Dix.

"Welcome to the U.S. Army," I thought.

It was beginning to get dark. I had to get back to the barracks and wasn't really sure where it was. I saw the guy who had been in front of me in the "Clinic" running down the street.

"He must know where he's going," I thought, and began running in the same direction remembering Decker's warning . . .

"TRAINEES DO NOT WALK!"

The new boots made a strange hollow sound as the heels hit the pavement. They weren't broken in and didn't fit right. The backs of them were rubbing against my heels.

"I'm going to get blisters on top of everything else," I thought.

"Just what I really need . . . blisters."

I ran past the barber shop. Things were beginning to look familiar.

Maybe it was its light that drew me to it. I don't know why I hadn't seen it before, but there it was; looking as out-of-place as I felt . . . a phone booth!

A real, honest to God, New Jersey Bell, telephone booth!

"I can call Janie; let her know I'm still alive."

I ran toward the light as fast as I could with the boots rubbing against my heels.

"It has to be quick . . ."

The door flung open as I grabbed its handle with both hands and pulled. I grabbed the receiver and punched the "O" for the operator.

"Operator . . ." Her voice sounded lethargic.

"I need to make a collect call to Clifton New Jersey . . . Quickly!"

"Did you say . . . Clifton?"

"Yes! Clifton New Jersey! . . . It's an Emergency!"

God, she was slow.

"May I have your name . . . and the number you wish to call?"

I gave her my name and Janie's number as another guy ran past the booth. His arms were bleeding too.

"Hello."

It was Janie's voice! . . . God, she sounded good!

"Will you accept a collect call from a Mr. Don Yost?"

"Yes . . . I'll accept the call."

"Janie!"

"Don! . . . Is that you?"

"Yes! . . . Its me! . . . I don't have much time . . . I just want you to know that I'm missing you . . . It's really something else here . . . You wouldn't believe it!"

"How are they treating you?" she asked.

"Like I said, . . . You wouldn't believe it . . . I'm standing here in a phone booth with blood running down both arms!"

"Blood! . . . What happened?"

"They just gave us our shots . . . It was brutal."

"Tell them to put something on it."

"Yeah, . . . O.K."

"If she only knew . . .," I thought.

"I'm really missing you," I told her.

"I miss you too," she said.

"Well . . . I have to go now, I'll call again as soon as I can . . . I love you."

"Me too."

"Her parents must be in the room," I thought. "That's why she didn't say 'I love you too.'

"Well . . . bye."

"Bye."

I waited for the dial tone before I hung up the phone. Janie seemed so far away. She might as well have been on the other side of the world. God, I felt alone without her. Talking with her over the phone seemed so cold. I wanted to hold her, not call her collect and talk to her with her parents in the room. Maybe I shouldn't have called . . .

"BANG!!!" . . . "BANG!!!" . . . "BANG!!!"

The telephone booth shook with the pounding!

My heart jumped as I spun around.

A DRILL SERGEANTS HAT! . . .

THE RED, BLOOD SHOT EYES! . . .

THE SQUARE, MEAN LOOKING JAW! . . .

DECKER!

"DROP!"

"I SAID . . . DROP!" he yelled.

I opened the door and dropped to the ground. My feet were still inside the booth.

"One . . . Sergeant! . . .

"Two . . . Sergeant! . . .

"Three . . . Sergeant! . . .

My chin touched the toe of his boot as I did each push-up. He didn't tell me how many to do and I wasn't going to ask him.

My shoulders were killing me. They still ached from the shots. Every push-up made them hurt more.

"Ten . . . Sergeant!

"Eleven . . . Sergeant!

Decker walked away, leaving me there counting pushups to myself.

"Twelve . . . Sergeant!

Scratchy music began playing from the public address system. "Taps" never seemed so appropriate. When it ended, I was still doing pushups.

"Twenty ... ... Two ... ... S . . . ."

I couldn't do any more . . . My shoulders hurt too much.

"Let him kill me." I thought as I stood up. I was exhausted.

I had barely enough energy left to make it to the barracks. Everyone else was already in their bunks. I stumbled to the one under Pruit, grabbed the clothes that I had left there, and stuffed them into the footlocker.

I un-rolled the mattress with one hand while I unbuttoned my fatigue shirt with the other. Finally I was in my underwear and collapsed on the bed.

"A . . . TIN . . . HUT!"

"Oh . . . Shit! . . ." I thought as I forced myself up off the bunk. Decker had stepped out of his own private room at the far end of the barracks. . . . He would be living with us for the entire eight weeks!

"LIGHTS OUT IN FIVE MINUTES! . . . THAT'S TWENTY-TWO HUNDRED HOURS! YOU WILL SLEEP AT ATTENTION!" He yelled.

Then he disappeared into his room and slammed the door closed. We climbed back into our bunks. Five minutes later, the lights were turned off.

I lay there in the dark with my shoulders throbbing and the backs of my heels burning, trying to blot-out all that had happened that day. The barracks filled with quiet born of exhaustion.

Suddenly the silence was broken by the faint sound of muffled crying. It sounded like a homesick kid on his first night of summer camp. I listened to it for a few minutes, trying to figure out who it was.

"Chuck . . ." I said in a quiet voice to the lump in the bedspring above me.

"Yeah?" He whispered back.

"What do you think?"

"What do you mean?" he asked.

"I mean . . . Do you think we might have made a mistake? . . ."

There was no response.

We lay there in the darkness, each lost in our own private thoughts, listening to the muffled crying.

Somehow, it seemed my question had been answered . . .

Chapter Eight

"War Doesn't Care"

We learned a lot about the Army and even more about ourselves in the weeks of training that followed. We learned that we were no longer human beings. We were being transformed into soldiers . . . objects . . . pieces of military hardware.

"Why is it that they're all Blacks?" Chuck asked.

The question came from nowhere. He was thinking out-loud.

"Huh?"

"The sergeants," he said. "I never saw so many black people in my life."

Most of the sergeants, the ones responsible for teaching us, were either Black or Puerto Rican.

"Where do you expect them to get jobs on the outside?" I asked him. "Do you think they'd be somebody's boss on the outside?"

"No, I guess not."

"So, what choice do they have? . . . The Army's their life."

"I guess you're right. They don't have much of a choice."

They were "Lifers": prisoners serving a life sentence with no chance of parole. They had all been to Vietnam at least once. Most had served two tours there.

It didn't seem right that they had to shoulder most of the burden. I wondered about that. I wondered about that a lot.

The Civil Rights Movement was at its peak. Americans, Black Americans were rioting in the streets of Washington and Los Angeles and Detroit, protesting school segregation. "Watts" and "Selma" weren't just names of places anymore. Now they were names of battlefields like "Gettysburg," "Mannassas," "Bull Run."

People were angry. They said they wanted "Freedom." They were being fought in the streets by police with teargas and German shepherds. Even the National Guard had been called up. America was at war with herself, fighting her own people.

And yet America was supposed to love freedom so much she was willing to fight a war on the other side of the world to defend it. She was even willing to sacrifice some of her own children . . . her stepchildren, those who were Black or Puerto Rican or poor white kids who couldn't afford a college deferment . . . the expendable ones who wouldn't be missed all that much . . . the ones who had no choice. It seemed so hypocritical. It bothered me.

Why were we in Vietnam? What was the real reason? It wasn't right to ask people to die for no reason, even if they were expendable, even if they wouldn't be missed. The America I thought I knew wouldn't do that.

The "Lifers" had a serious attitude. When they yelled at us it wasn't to break us down, it was because we had done something wrong, something they were sure would get us killed . . . killed in Vietnam.

They had no doubt we were headed there and it was their job to help us live through it. They were like parents teaching their children, doing their best to prepare us for what was coming.

They had seen it. They had walked through the gates of hell and peered into its fiery abyss. The journey had changed them.

"Today, people, you will go through the Confidence Course." Sergeant Perez told us one cold December morning. (There is nowhere on earth as cold as Fort Dix in December.)

He paced slowly in front of us with his hands clasped behind his back. He looked directly into our eyes as he spoke. His words were slow, deliberate, intense.

"You will follow commands without question. . . . You will be careful. . . . Is that understood?"

"Yes . . . Sergeant!"

He nodded his head, glad that we understood.

"The Confidence Course will teach you that you are able to do things, things you never thought you could do. It will teach you to deal with fear."

The sergeant's dark eyes had a distant look, like he was remembering something, something that had happened in another lifetime on a distant planet, in another galaxy . . . something that still lived somewhere deep in the recesses of his soul.

We had seen that look in his eyes before. "The thousand-yard stare" they called it. All Vietnam Veterans had that look about them and it made us nervous.

The "Confidence Course" was a series of obstacles. There were rope ladders to climb, walls to scale and barbed wire to crawl under. It looked like a challenge physically, but none of it seemed frightening. I didn't understand what he meant, saying it would teach us "to deal with fear."

"This doesn't look so bad, Chuck . . ."

There was a pause before he answered.

"Wait 'til the machine guns open up . . ."

"Machine guns? . . . What machine guns?"

"Those machine guns" he said, and pointed toward the barbed wire.

"They're going to be shooting real bullets over us while we crawl under the wire."

I looked in the direction he was pointing. They had set two machine guns at one end of the field.

"So what? . . . They're not going to try to kill us; they won't be aiming at us. What can happen?"

"You're comfortable, trusting your life to those idiots?" he asked. "I heard some guy got killed doing this."

"Well what did he do, stand up or something stupid like that?"

"Well, yeah. . . . I guess so. They said he saw a snake or something. . . ."

"Well then, what do you expect? The guy was a jerk, that's all, just a jerk. It's too cold for snakes anyway. This won't be so bad."

Chuck shook his head at me. He wasn't convinced.

They lined us up in rows at one end of the field facing the guns.

"List'n up!," Perez shouted.

"When I give the command, you will drop and get on your backs . . . on your backs . . . do you understand?"

"Yes, Sergeant!"

He wasn't satisfied and told Murphy to demonstrate. Murphy got on his back.

"Hold your rifle across your chest . . . like this, so it doesn't get caught. Then push yourself with your legs so you slide under the wire."

He made Murphy show us how to do it.

"All right, drop!"

We dropped to the ground and rolled over onto our backs.

"Now make sure you stay in your lanes and be careful."

A few minutes passed before a crackling voice from a loud-speaker gave the order for us to "Move out."

We pushed ourselves under the wire. I could feel the cold ground through my field jacket. The weight of the M-14 rifle pressed down on my chest. It was heavy and clumsy.

I had never seen barbed wire up-close before. It was ugly, sil-houetted against the gray sky, its barbs looking like they wanted to tear your eyes out. They had a cold, brutal personality to them.

"Blood thirsty vultures," I thought.

I wondered about the guy who'd invented barbed wire. What kind of sadist must he have been? I pictured him at work, bald and thin with wire-rimmed glasses.

"Just how far apart should the barbs be placed? . . ." he must have thought.

"Exactly how sharp should I make them so they'll tear flesh? . . ."

"What gauge wire should I use? . . ."

"It has to be strong enough . . . strong enough to hold the dead weight. . . ."

I wondered if he had any kids. I wondered if he went to church. I wondered how he was able to live with himself.

I pushed myself under the first strand of wire and heard a shrill whistling sound. Suddenly an explosion no more than five feet away shook the ground under me.

My entire body flinched and the acrid smell of sulphur burned my nostrils.

Now I understood . . . I understood why Perez told us to stay in our lanes . . . There were simulators between them. They made it seem like an invisible enemy was firing mortars or artillery at us.

"I'm getting through this quickly . . . as fast as I can . . .," I thought.

I looked over at the guy in the lane next to me. The sleeve of his field jacket had gotten caught on the wire and he was frantically trying to free it.

Another shrill whistle. . . .

Another explosion. . . .

They were "coming in" faster now. There were explosions all around us.

"STAY . . . IN . . . YOUR . . . LANES! . . . STAY . . . IN . . . YOUR . . . LANES!" The voice of the loudspeaker crackled.

I think that's what it said. I could barely hear it over the explosions.

My legs seemed to be moving by themselves. The heels of my boots slid on the frozen ground. I couldn't get any traction like a turtle; helpless on its back.

"I'm not moving! . . . Just great! . . . This is just great!"

More whistles. . . .

More explosions. . . .

I let go of the rifle and let it rest by itself across my chest so I could use my forearms and elbows to push.

"This is ridiculous . . .," I thought as I strained to look over my shoulder to see where I was going. It was a helpless feeling, being trapped under the wire. The field jacket felt huge and heavy, like it was five sizes too big, holding me back, slowing me down.

"There's no going back now." I thought, "God . . ." What if this was for real . . ."

I got to the second strand of wire just as the machine guns roared. They had a deep, rumbling sound to them, like two '59 Cadillacs that needed mufflers. The sky was crisscrossed with bright orange lines . . . tracer bullets.

I could hear them cut through the air. It seemed like they were no more than three feet above me, like I could reach up and touch them, like stars on a clear, summer night.

I wondered how it would feel to get hit by a tracer. . . . Would it get inside you and burn there for a while?

Another explosion . . .

"Oh, Man! . . . that was close! . . . Stay in the lane . . . Stay in the lane . . ."

As I moved back to the center of the lane, the rifle slid off my chest and fell to the ground. I put it back on top of me and kept moving.

"Thank God it's not loaded. . . ."

The guy next to me had finally freed himself from the wire and was trying to make up the time he'd lost. His helmet had fallen off and he shoved it back on his head, holding it there with one hand. His legs were moving in all directions as he tried to catch up with the rest of us. I wondered if I looked that pathetic.

A shrill whistle. . . .

An explosion. . . .

The field was shrouded in smoke now; the smell of gunpowder was so thick, I could taste it. It was a smell I would never forget.

By the time I was half-way across the field, something had happened. I no longer felt anything . . . absolutely nothing.

It was strange; as if a circuit breaker inside of me had tripped, turning off the ability to feel emotions. It had happened automatically, without my realizing it. Maybe that's what the sergeant meant when he said we would learn to "deal with fear."

I don't know how long I was under the wire and bullets. Somehow, I must have gotten across the field. I found myself standing behind the machine-guns, bent over with my hands on my knees. I was staring at my boots, out of breath and exhausted. A minute later, the guns were silent and the explosions had stopped.

"We would have never made it. . . . There's no way we could have made it."

Chuck was out of breath and his voice sounded strange . . . far away . . . like in a dream. His words had a matter-of-fact tone to them like an accountant analyzing a profit and loss statement.

"What do you mean?" I asked him after I caught my breath and could speak again. He was looking back toward the wire.

"We'd have never made it. If they were trying to kill us . . . we'd be dead now."

I looked back at the empty field and pictured it filled with distorted, dead bodies. They hung in grotesque positions on the barbed wire . . . a field of crucifixes, shrouded in smoke.

"War doesn't care," I thought. "It doesn't care who's good or who's bad . . . who's right or who's wrong . . . who deserves to live or who deserves to die. It just destroys everything."

I thought about the guy who got his sleeve caught. He would've been killed the instant the machine-guns opened up. He wouldn't have stood a chance.

He would have been killed not because he believed in Democracy, not because he wanted to free oppressed people, nothing so noble as that.

He would be dead because he got the sleeve of his jacket caught in the wire.

"He died for God and Country. He was a hero." They would have told his mother as they handed her a folded American flag.

They would never have told the truth: "He was killed because he got his sleeve caught in the wire."

That would be too meaningless, too impersonal.

"War . . . doesn't care," I said.

"What?"

"War just doesn't care," I repeated.

I don't know if Chuck understood what I meant, but he nodded his head anyway as if maybe he did. . . .

Chapter Nine

"You Don't Belong Here"

It was January of 1968 and something was happening in Vietnam; something the newspapers were calling "The Tet Offensive."

The Vietcong and NVA had launched a massive attack. Every American position was being hit and hit hard. There were stories about a place where the Marines were getting torn apart, a strange-sounding place called "Khe Sanh."

Khe Sanh was being compared to the battle of Dhin Bien Phu. The French had lost a battle there years ago and had finally pulled out of Vietnam, giving it up as a lost cause. They said Khe Sanh was our Dhin Bien Phu, a turning point of the war. It wasn't winding down. We were losing.

The anti-war protests in America were turning bitter and ugly. They were burning the flag in the streets of Washington. Guys coming back from Vietnam weren't welcomed. They were being greeted by mobs of college students who called them "Baby Killers" and even spit on them.

It had become fashionable for college kids to do that. They thought they were "Intellectuals." They thought they knew so much. They saw themselves as heroes, taking a stand against the "Establishment." It was easy to be a "hero" when Daddy's money had bought you a college deferment.

They called themselves "Flower Children" and said they wanted people to "LOV" one another. I wondered if they even knew what "Lov" meant. They didn't spell the word correctly, and it didn't seem particularly loving to spit in the face of a 19-year-old who had just lost his legs in Vietnam.

The four of us stood there, stranded outside the brick, two-story building that looked like a school. We were late, they told us.

Class #96 of Officer Candidate School had already begun. That wasn't good.

We'd arrived at Fort Benning a week earlier, but they kept us hanging around until they could get their classes organized. Chuck was assigned to a class right away with most of the others. They started O.C.S. two days before and we were the last four to be assigned.

"They're going to treat you like candidates," the sergeant was warning us.

"It would have been better if you started with the rest of the class. Now, you're going to get special attention."

His voice had an ominous tone to it. I didn't like the sound of it.

"It's not our fault we're late," I thought.

I remembered Sergeant Decker from Basic training. I wondered if it was going to be like that, if they were going to try to break us again. They would have six months to mess with our minds in O.C.S. I imagined it would be a long six months.

"It's gonna be tough," he continued. "Half the class won't make it through, but if you want it bad enough, if you really want to be platoon leaders, you'll make it."

"Wait a minute!" I thought. "Only half the class makes it through? . . . Only half?"

Sergeant Thomas didn't tell me that half the guys going to O.C.S. didn't make it.

"And what's this about wanting to be a platoon leader? Who wants to be a platoon leader?"

I wondered what else Thomas hadn't told me.

"What have I gotten myself into? . . ."

Janie and I had set our wedding date for July 13th. O.C.S. would be over by then and I would be an Officer. Everything would be messed up if I didn't make it. Everything was planned. I hadn't even considered the possibility of being washed out.

"I have to make it. . . ."

I thought the pressure would help. No matter what, I had to make it through O.C.S.

"Sergeant?" one of the guys asked.

"Yeah?"

"What happens if we don't make it?"

I thought it was an excellent question. We stood there in silence, waiting . . . afraid of what he might say.

The sergeant didn't answer right away. He nodded his head as if he had heard the question before.

"Well, if you don't make it, or if you drop out, they'll send you to Vietnam."

His words ricocheted off the building's brick walls and echoed back at us.

"They'll send you to Vietnam. . . ." It rang in our ears like a death sentence.

There was no doubt in his voice, none at all. It was a statement of fact.

I felt sick. I glanced at the guy standing next to me. His face had turned pale.

"Did you say *Vietnam*? . . ." The first guy asked again as if the sergeant wasn't clear, hoping he'd misunderstood.

"That's right. You get thirty days off and then they send you over."

"But they told me I was going to be an Administration Officer . . . an Administration Officer in Germany." His voice sounded weak and pathetic.

The sergeant looked down at the ground and shook his head.

"Well, what's your M . . . O . . . S.?" he asked, still looking at the ground. There was a smirk on his face. He already knew the answer.

"My M.O.S.?"

"Yeah, your Military Occupational Specialty. Did you forget what your M.O.S. *is*?"

"No, I didn't forget."

"Well, what is it?"

"It's . . . Eleven Bravo Twenty. . . ."

"And what's Eleven Bravo Twenty mean . . . ?"

There was a long pause as the realization dawned. He didn't want to say the word. I didn't want to hear him say it. I closed my eyes hoping it would all go away like a patient in a dentist's chair seeing the syringe, knowing this was going to hurt.

When the answer came, it was a whimper . . . a helpless, hopeless, whimper.

"Infantry. . . ."

The sergeant raised his head and looked him in the eyes.

"That's right," he said. "Infantry!"

I remembered Sergeant Thomas' smiling face.

"He knew. He knew all along. This can't be happening," I thought.

I felt like I had fallen into a raging river. There was nothing I could do to stop it. Everything I had hoped for, all the plans I had made for me and Janie were being washed away in the current.

Maybe there was still hope. Maybe this sergeant was just trying to shake us up. Maybe it was just part of the game. Maybe he didn't know what he was talking about.

There was such a thing as the Adjutant General Corps, wasn't there? Maybe he had never heard of it, but there was such a thing. Even if it didn't have it's own M.O.S., people still got into the Adjutant General Corps, didn't they? There was a brochure for it, wasn't there? I saw it, didn't I?

"That's it," I thought. "He's just trying to shake us up. He doesn't know what he's talking about. I just have to make it through the next six months and everything will work out."

I was drowning and grasping for straws.

"Now remember," the sergeant continued, "they're going to treat you like candidates."

Then he turned and walked away, leaving us standing there with our thoughts, wondering what was going to happen to us.

Twenty minutes of hell passed slowly as we stood there waiting for it to begin, wishing it wouldn't.

"BANG!! . . ."

The screen door of the building was suddenly kicked open.

Their boots were spit shined and their fatigue uniforms were starched stiff. The collars of their shirts had infantry crossed rifle insignia on them. Their shiny, black helmets, pulled low over their eyes, displayed a single gold bar. There were five of them. They were second lieutenants, our "Tach Officers."

They surrounded us and stood there with their hands on their hips looking us over. Their expressions said they were disgusted with what they saw.

"Attention!" One of them yelled. It seemed strange that he didn't say "A . . . Tin . . . Hut!"

"Things are going to be different here," I thought.

We snapped to attention as they prowled around us.

A minute or two passed before hell broke loose.

"ARE YOU EYEBALLIN' ME, CANDIDATE?!" One of them yelled at the guy who said he was told he would be an Administration Officer.

"No, Sergeant!."

I knew it was over for him. How could he be so dumb?

"SERGEANT?! . . . DID YOU CALL ME SERGEANT?!" the Lieutenant screamed.

He was taking this as a personal insult, like the guy had spit in his mother's face. He ran over and stood directly in front of him.

"DID YOU CALL ME 'SERGEANT,' CANDIDATE?!"

"No, Sergeant. I mean, no . . . Sir!"

"WHAT'S YOUR NAME, CANDIDATE?!" he yelled.

"Palmer," the guy mumbled.

"PALMER . . . WHAT?!"

"Palmer . . . Sir!"

"WHEN YOU ARE SPOKEN TO, YOU WILL SAY: 'SIR! . . . CANDIDATE PALMER, . . . YES SIR!,' OR, 'SIR! . . . CANDIDATE PALMER, . . . NO SIR!,' . . . DO YOU UNDERSTAND, CANDIDATE?!"

"Sir! . . . Candidate Palmer . . . Yes Sir!"

"DROP AND GIVE ME TWENTY!"

Palmer dropped to the push-up position and began doing his penance.

"Sir! . . . Candidate Palmer . . . One, Sir!"

"Sir! . . . Candidate Palmer . . . Two, Sir!"

"Sir! . . . Candidate Palmer . . . Three, Sir!"

The rest of us tried our best to keep our eyes straight ahead. One of the officers was suddenly in front of me. His hands were clasped behind his back and he was studying my boots. I hadn't polished them.

He was tall and thin and his angular face was rutted with deep acne scars. His eyes were small and piercing . . . the eyes of a snake.

He was much older than the others, maybe in his late twenties. He must have been in the Army for a while. Now he was fresh out of O.C.S., a brand new "Butter Bar Lieutenant" with an axe to grind.

He reminded me of a high-school wiseguy . . . a punk, the type who wore their leather jackets with the collar up and rode motorcycles. They were older than the other kids in highschool. They should have already graduated but their grades kept them back. They ruled the school hallway with fear and bullied the younger kids for their lunch money.

I hated Lieutenant Rice from the moment I saw him.

He read my name tag.

His thick lips formed a sarcastic grin like the bully crushing his cigarette just before he slams his victim against a locker.

"What's a . . . . Y . . . o . . st?"

He said my name in a slow, drawl like he smelled something; like it was a dirty word.

"Sir! . . . Candidate Yost! . . . It's my name . . . Sir!"

"DID YOU GO TO COLLEGE . . . Y . . . ost?"

He yelled all the words except for my name. He said that like he had just stepped in dogshit.

Somehow I knew he had never gone to college.

"Sir . . . Candidate Yost . . . Yes Sir!"

"ARE YOU A FLOWER CHILD . . . YOST?!!"

He screamed the words at me. I kept my eyes riveted to the front. His spit hit my face.

"Sir! . . . Candidate Yost . . . No Sir!"

He went back to studying my boots and walked slowly around me to see what else was wrong. He put his scarred face close to my left ear.

"You don't belong here . . . Y . . . ost."

He whispered it like it was a secret, just between him and me as if he was telling me my fly was open.

They continued the abuse for thirty minutes. It reminded me of basic training except their attacks were more direct, more personal, like what Murphy went through because his hair was too long.

BANG!!!

The screen door was ripped from all but its top hinge this time. It stayed open, unable to close itself. It had been wounded, forced to surrender.

Standing in the open doorway at the top of the stairs was a completely bald Infantry Captain with huge ears. The Tach Officers stopped yelling at us and looked toward him.

He was stocky, almost overweight. He had a thick neck and the face of a bull. The sleeves of his shirt were rolled up to his shoulders. His hairless arms were massive, too big for the rest of his body. His hands were on his hips and he was angry . . . really angry.

In his right hand he held some sort of billyclub. He stood there looking at us for a moment. Then he spread his feet and began smacking the palm of his left hand with the club like he was thinking about beating someone to death with it.

It made a dull thump each time it struck his hand.

Thump, . . . thump, . . . thump. . . .

It was the rhythm of a heartbeat.

The club was white and about two feet long. It had a strange shape, bigger at both ends and narrow in the middle. I looked closer at it. It took a moment before the shock hit me, before I realized what it was.

He was holding a souvenir from Vietnam . . . a human leg bone.

Chapter Ten

"Janie Must Have Heard It, Too"

"Thump. . . ."

The heartbeat continued. . . .

One of the officers turned toward us.

"WHEN I POINT AT YOU, YOU WILL STEP FORWARD AND SALUTE THE CAPTAIN!"

"YOU WILL STATE YOUR NAME AND THE BRANCH OF THE ARMY TO WHICH YOU EXPECT TO BE ASSIGNED!."

"Thump. . . ."

"There's hope . . .," I thought. "There are other choices besides Infantry. . . ."

The lieutenant pointed to the guy on the end. He stepped forward and saluted. I expected the captain to return the salute but he didn't. He kept hitting the palm of his hand with the leg bone.

"Thump. . . ."

"Sir! . . . Candidate Bowers! . . . Infantry Sir!"

"What an idiot!" I thought, "Why would he want to be in the Infantry?"

Bowers finished his salute and took a step backward.

"Thump. . . ."

The tach officer pointed at Palmer, the guy who told the sergeant he wanted to be an "Administration Officer," whatever that was.

"Sir! . . . Candidate Palmer . . . Infantry . . . Sir!"

"Did he say . . . 'Infantry'!?"

"Thump. . . ."

They scared him into saying it. It only took them thirty minutes to break him, just thirty minutes.

Palmer got back in line, knowing it had all become hopeless, knowing he had given up. I felt sorry for him.

"Thump. . . ."

The lieutenant pointed at the guy standing next to me, the one who turned pale when the sergeant said we were going to Vietnam.

"Sir! . . . Candidate Wasniewski . . . Infantry Sir!"

"Thump. . . ."

"Him too?"

The tach officer pointed in my direction as Wasniewski got back in line.

"It's time," I thought.

I stepped forward and saluted.

"Thump. . . ."

I looked directly at the captain.

"SIR! CANDIDATE YOST! ADJUTANT GENERAL CORPS! . . . SIR!"

The heartbeat stopped. . . .

There was a long pause. . . .

An eternal "moment of silence."

The only sound was a feeble moan from the wounded door as it writhed in pain, reminding me of Palmer.

I could see Lieutenant Rice from the corner of my eye. He had a broad smirk on his face.

When the Captain spoke, his voice began with the low rumble of a volcano. . . .

"What. . . . did. . . . you. . . . say . . . ?!"

I repeated it, loud enough for the entire universe to hear . . . My final act of defiance.

"SIR! . . . CANDIDATE YOST! . . . ADJUTANT GENERAL CORPS . . . SIR!"

The building's brick walls mimicked my voice and shouted the words back at me.

I sounded ridiculous.

The volcano erupted. . . .

"THEY DID IT . . . AGAIN!" the captain shouted.

"THEY DID IT . . . TO ME . . . AGAIN!"

He was looking for something to kill.

He turned toward the screen door and kicked it. Then he kicked it again.

"GODDAMN . . . FLOWER CHILDREN!"

"THEY'RE SENDING ME GODDAMN FLOWER CHIL-DREN!"

The screen door died and fell from its frame. Its corpse crashed to the foot of the steps and lay there, no longer in pain, finally at peace.

Unsatiated by his kill, the captain turned and stormed inside the building, cursing the beaurocrats who had sent him "flower children."

"You are sorry . . . Y . . . ost," Rice whispered.

I got back in line.

"LIST'N UP!" The first Tach Officer yelled, "THE DOOR TO THE MESS HALL IS ON YOUR RIGHT. YOU WILL DO TEN PULL-UPS ON THE BAR OVER THE DOOR BEFORE YOU ENTER THE MESS HALL!."

The bar was higher than it should have been. We had to jump as high as we could to reach it. Bowers jumped to grab it and missed. He jumped a second time, grabbed the bar and started his pull-ups.

"Sir! . . . Candidate Bowers . . . One . . . Sir!

"Sir! . . . Candidate Bowers . . . Two . . . Sir!"

He lost his grip and fell from the bar.

"GET TO THE END OF THE LINE, CANDIDATE!"

Bowers got on line behind me and Palmer grabbed the bar.

"Sir! . . . Candidate Palmer . . . One . . . Sir!"

Each time one of us fell from the bar, they forced him to go to the end of the line. We finally finished the pull-ups and stood waiting outside the door of the mess hall.

"LIST'N UP!" Rice yelled.

"YOU WILL MARCH INTO THE MESS HALL AND GET YOUR CHOW. YOU WILL EAT AT ATTENTION!

"YOUR BACK WILL NOT TOUCH THE CHAIR!

"YOU WILL KEEP YOUR EYES TO THE FRONT AT ALL TIMES! YOUR FEET WILL BE FLAT ON THE FLOOR!

"YOUR FORK WILL BE ON THE RIGHT SIDE OF YOUR TRAY! YOU WILL RAISE YOUR FORK STRAIGHT UP ABOVE THE TRAY AND WILL BRING IT TO YOUR MOUTH AT A RIGHT ANGLE!

"YOUR FORK WILL FOLLOW THE SAME RIGHT ANGLE FROM YOUR MOUTH BACK DOWN TO THE TRAY AFTER EACH MOUTHFUL!

"YOU WILL REST YOUR FORK AGAINST THE TRAY AND WILL KEEP YOUR HANDS FOLDED IN YOUR LAP AS YOU CHEW!

"YOU WILL CHEW EACH MOUTHFUL OF FOOD TWENTY TIMES BEFORE SWALLOWING!"

The door of the mess hall opened and we marched inside. We got our metal trays of food and carried them to the table. I sat on the edge of the chair so I wouldn't touch its back.

With my eyes to the front, I tried to get something on the fork without looking down at the tray.

"This is impossible. . . ."

I lifted the fork to my mouth at a right angle. There was nothing on it.

"Just great. . . ."

I brought the fork back down to the tray and chewed as if there was food in my mouth.

"YOU EYEBALLIN' YOUR FOOD, CANDIDATE?!" Rice yelled at Wasniewski.

"Sir! . . . Candidate Wasniewski! . . . No Sir!"

"STAND AT ATTENTION WHEN YOU ARE ADDRESSED BY AN OFFICER!"

Wasniewski stood up. I kept my eyes to the front, continuing to pretend I was eating. It couldn't see anything except the wall directly in front of me.

I heard the door open and the sound of shuffling feet.

"It must be the rest of the class."

I raised the fork and was about to bring it to my mouth when I felt someone's hot breath on my neck.

"YOU REALLY EATING THAT FOOD . . . CANDIDATE!?"

He yelled it in my right ear, loud enough to make it hurt.

"Sir! . . . Candidate Yost! . . . Yes Sir!"

"STAND AT ATTENTION WHEN YOU ARE ADDRESSED BY A SENIOR CANDIDATE!"

I put the fork down slowly, making sure to follow the path of the right angle, stood and turned to face him.

The room was filled with guys wearing shiny, black helmets with blue O.C.S. emblems on the front. There must have been fifty of them.

They wore ascots pulled high to their chins. The light blue color meant they were in the Infantry.

This wasn't the rest of class "Ninety-Six," these were "Senior Candidates" from some other class.

They were almost ready to graduate. It was their turn to give back some of the abuse they had taken . . . six months of pent-up rage to dump on somebody . . . anybody.

They needed victims. They needed victims desperately and there were only four of us.

Their hungry eyes showed their disappointment. We were a mere tidbit, a morsel . . . a crumb.

We would have to do.

The messhall seemed an appropriate place for them to devour us. They were about to begin feasting when someone yelled.

"CHOW'S OVER! . . . TAKE THEM INTO THE "DAY-ROOM!"

The "Dayroom" was huge and empty except for a few uphol-stered chairs covered with plastic. The walls were lined with striped drapes.

The torment began immediately. They all began shouting at once. I found myself in the center of a circle, surrounded by ten of them.

"WHERE ARE YOU FROM, CANDIDATE!?" One of them screamed in a thick southern accent, his spit hitting my face.

"Sir! . . . Candidate Yost! . . . New Jersey . . . Sir!"

I fixed my eyes on the drapes so that I wouldn't "eyeball" any-thing. The lines of their striped pattern seemed to be moving.

"NEW JOI . . . SEY!" another scoffed, "DID YOU SAY NEW JOI . . . SEY, CANDIDATE?"

"Sir! . . . Candidate Yost! . . . Yes Sir!"

"NEW . . . JOISEY! . . . another yelled, "THAT PLACE SMELLS BAD . . . DOESN'T IT, CANDIDATE!?"

"Sir! . . . Candidate Yost! . . . No Sir!

"THAT'S WHERE NEW YORK DUMPS ITS GARBAGE! . . .
YOU A PIECE OF GARBAGE FROM . . . JOISEY, CANDI-
DATE?"

"KEEP YOUR EYES TO THE FRONT!" Another yelled from
behind me before I could answer.

"I ASKED YOU IF YOU'RE A PIECE OF . . . GARBAGE!"

I felt more spit hit my face.

"Sir! . . . Candidate Yost! . . . NO SIR!"

The lines on the drapes kept moving. I strained my eyes to
make them stop. They started to blur.

"DID YOU GO TO COLLEGE, . . . CANDIDATE?"

The voice came from somewhere on my left, it sounded black.

"Sir! . . . Candidate Yost! . . . Yes Sir!"

"WHAT WAS YOUR MAJOR, CANDIDATE?"

"Sir! . . . Candidate Yost! . . . English Literature . . . Sir!"

It sounded incredibly stupid. "English Literature" had no place
at all here. It sounded like a girl's major. I wished I hadn't said it.

The drapes had become a total blur and the room started spin-
ning. I rubbed my eyes with my shirt sleeve. The movement was all
the piranha needed, everything they had been waiting for. The ten of
them began fighting over the last morsel of flesh.

I couldn't understand what they were saying. I heard only bits
and pieces of sentences . . . individual, disconnected words . . .

"JOISEY!" . . . "EYEBALL!" . . . "ENGLISH!" . . .
"DUFUS!" . . . "COLLEGE!" . . . "SORRY!" . . . "FLOWER
CHILD!" . . . "GARBAGE!"

It was like standing in a snake pit. I felt their hot venom hit
my face and neck as they struck. I tried to be still so they wouldn't
attack, but it wasn't working.

I stood there without speaking, not trying to answer, silently
staring at the ugly, blurred, striped drapes.

"YOST!"

It was Rice's shout that brought an end to the feeding frenzy.

"THE CAPTAIN WANTS YOU! . . . IN HIS OFFICE! . . .
A.S.A.P.!"

Their yelling stopped. They reluctantly stepped aside and allowed me to leave the pit. They weren't finished.

I looked at Rice. He was pointing to the hallway. I guessed that's where the Captain's office was and ran toward it.

"Now what?" I thought, "What does the Captain want with me? Maybe it's good. Maybe it's about the Adjutant General Corps. . . ."

I found an office with the Captain's name on it. Like Dorothy in the Land of Oz, I pounded on the Wizard's door, hoping he knew the way back to Kansas.

"ENTER!"

The Wizard was still angry.

I opened the heavy door and stepped inside.

He sat behind a huge, mahogany desk. There were no files on it. Its polished top was completely empty.

He looked strange sitting behind the empty desk, and yet, the scene was somehow familiar.

It took me a moment before I made the connection, before I realized why it seemed this had happened before.

"A priest . . .," I thought, "A priest behind the altar, preparing to say Mass . . . about to offer the sacrifice."

There was no crucifix behind the altar. Instead, painted on the wall, were two crossed rifles. Beneath the rifles in huge black letters were the words:

"INFANTRY! . . . SIR!"

It read like a newspaper headline. Suddenly I knew it was hopeless.

I came to attention and saluted. It seemed as though I should have genuflected.

"SIR! . . . CANDIDATE YOST! . . . REPORTING AS OR-DERED SIR!"

The Captain didn't return my salute. He let me stand there staring at the wall, feeling stupid, waiting for something to happen.

"BANG!!"

He pounded both fists at once on the top of the altar, forcing me to blink.

"BANG!!"

He pounded the altar harder this time.

I looked right at him. His eyes were bulging. His face had turned a bright red. The veins of his thick neck were about to burst.

His huge arms lifted him mechanically from the chair, like a fork-lift truck. He leaned forward across the desk so that his face was only inches away from mine.

Then he bellowed. He bellowed the humiliating words I would never forget.

"ARE YOU . . . CRYING . . . BOY?! . . .

"ARE YOU . . . CRYING?! . . . IN MY DAYROOM?!"

It was loud enough so everyone could hear it.

It echoed down the hall and through the day room.

It echoed through the mess-hall.

It echoed out of the building and passed the lifeless body of the murdered screen door.

It echoed from the recruiter's office in the Paterson Post Office.

It echoed from my uncle Frank's statue in Fort Dix and from his flag-draped casket in my grandmother's livingroom.

And wherever she was, whatever she was doing, on that morning in January, 1968, somehow I felt that Janie must have heard it too . . .

Chapter Eleven

"I'm Sorry, Janie"

"We're gonna Rape . . . Rape . . .
Plunder . . . Plunder . . .
Pillage and Burn . . ."

"We're gonna Rape . . . Rape . . .
Plunder . . . Plunder . . .
Pillage and Burn . . ."

It was sick . . . just sick.

I pretended to yell the words of the cadence the others shouted as we marched, but I couldn't actually say the words. They disgusted me.

We were training to be "Officers." We were supposed to be the best America had to offer and we were singing about how we were going to "Rape, plunder and burn." I wanted to vomit.

I should have been farther along. I was supposed to hate . . . something . . . by now. All I hated was the Army and Lieutenant Rice. Five months had passed and what was left of class Ninety-six was going to "Turn blue," become "Senior Candidates" in less than a week. Half the class had dropped out and had been sent to Vietnam as punishment.

I wondered how Chuck Pruit was doing, if he was still alive. Somebody told me he had been assigned to class Ninety-six too and lasted only three days.

"Only three days?!" I'd asked in disbelief.

"Yeah," they told me. "It was brutal. Rice forced him to do whistle drills until he dropped."

We hated "whistle drills." They were torture disguised as exercise.

When the Tach Officer blew his whistle once, it meant . . . "Push-ups."

Two whistles . . . "Run in place."

Three whistles . . . "Jumping jacks."

Four whistles . . . "Sit ups."

The whistles came in rapid bursts like machine gun fire. The executioners stopped before it got dangerous; before they damaged government property. But Rice didn't know when to stop. He liked this part of his job. He liked it too much.

He'd continued the torment day and night with no let-up. He would storm into Chuck's room at two or three in the morning, screaming . . .

"YOU DON'T BELONG HERE, PRUIT! . . . YOU ARE WORTHLESS! . . . DO YOUR COUNTRY A FAVOR, PRUIT! . . . DROP OUT! . . . DROP OUT, PRUIT!"

The humiliation had been intense, perverted and insane and it had been effective.

"At the end, Pruit couldn't remember his own name," they said.

After three days, Chuck and three other guys dropped out. When they quit, Rice forced them to stand in front of the class and say they didn't have what it took to be Officers. It explained how there was room for the four of us who reported "late." I had been given Chuck's place.

He was somewhere in Vietnam now, not a good place for a "Pillsbury Doughboy" from Rutgers. I hoped he was all right.

The Captain called us to attention when we got back to the barracks.

"List'n up! Lieutenant Swann got some good news this morning. He wants to tell you about it."

Lieutenant Swann was a Tach Officer, but he wasn't anything like Rice. He looked like a blonde-haired school kid: tall, thin and unsure of himself. His face was ghostly pale and he was nervous.

"Like the Captain said, I got some good news this morning. . . ."

He mumbled the words. It was hard to hear him. Whatever the "good news" was, he didn't look happy about it.

"Sound off, Lieutenant!" the Captain yelled.

"Sorry Sir . . ."

His voice was a little stronger, but it was still difficult to hear. His head was bowed and he seemed to be speaking to the toes of his dusty, black boots.

"I got some good news this morning. . . ."

He hesitated.

"It's everything . . ."

He took a deep breath.

"It's everything I've worked for. It's everything . . ."

He sighed the words.

". . . everything I've been trained for . . ."

The Captain shifted his weight from one foot to the other and thumped the palm of his hand hard with the leg bone.

"Get on with it, Lieutenant!"

"Yes, Sir. . . . Sorry, Sir. . . ."

Lieutenant Swann gathered his thoughts. Then the words rushed out of him like flood water bursting through a dam.

"I got my orders. I'm going to Vietnam. I'll be a Platoon Leader. I'm not afraid. . . ."

He wrung his hands as he spoke. Drops of sweat formed on his forehead and trickled into his eyes. He looked like a condemned criminal waiting for the executioner's footsteps.

Rice stood to one side. His hands were clasped behind his back and he was looking directly at me. He was enjoying it. His thick lips formed the familiar smirk as he rocked slowly back and forth on those skinny, bowed legs of his. I stared into his pock-marked face and wished to hell he was going to Vietnam.

"I've had the best training in the world," Swann continued. "I've prepared for whatever happens."

He was trying to convince himself, but he was failing miserably. He knew, we all knew, that the training wasn't going to be enough. We'd spent the last five months studying technical equipment manuals. I still couldn't read a map and they'd given us only one demonstration of how to call in an artillery fire mission. We didn't even know how to use a field radio.

And we all knew that Infantry Platoon Leaders had the highest casualty rate in Vietnam. They called them "cannon fodder." It meant "expendable."

We waited while Swann tried to think of something else to say about his "good news." When he finally spoke, his words sounded hollow, rehearsed and stupid.

"I look forward to serving my Country in her hour of need. . . ."

It had all been said. It was over. Swann was finished.

"Well, what are you waiting for?" the Captain yelled at us. "Congratulate the Lieutenant!"

We cheered, sort of. It was a forced cheer, a stupid cheer, a moan.

If it had been Rice, it would have been different. I would have cheered his going to Vietnam and I would have relished it. But it wasn't Rice. It was Lieutenant Swann and that made a difference. He was one of us.

It was sad, watching him turn and slowly walk away with his shoulders slouched and head bowed like a ghost walking ahead of us into the future. Even the unit patch on his sleeve, the patch we all wore at Fort Benning, bemoaned our future with the hopeless voice of a Dickens spirit.

The patch was light blue . . . "Infantry Blue." Against its blue background was a picture of a bayonet and inscribed above the bayonet, like an epitaph on a tombstone, were the foreboding words . . . "Follow Me."

The ghost of Lieutenant Swann turned a corner and was suddenly gone.

I didn't want to follow him. I didn't want to take the road he was taking, but there was no option. It was clear now. We were all going to Vietnam.

"Company dismissed!" The Captain yelled.

"That does it," Bull said in a low voice as we stepped through the barracks doorway. "I'm writing my Congressman again. I've had it."

"Bull's" real name was "Trumbauer" and we shared the same room. He had the thick neck and massive shoulders of a football defensive lineman. He'd played for Oklahoma and I liked him. We all liked him. He was genuine and honest, one of those people who would do anything for you, a gentle giant.

"What's your Congressman going to do?" I asked him. "He didn't answer your other letters."

"He will. . . . He has to."

"But there's no time, Bull. There's only a month left."

"He'll do something."

When we got to our room, Bull grabbed the doorknob and tried to turn it. It didn't move.

"Locked! . . . It's locked! . . ."

We knew what it meant. Rice had "blitzed" the room.

"They're not supposed to be doing this to us now!" Bull said. "We're almost Senior Candidates."

It was a bad sign. Rice was telling us something. He wasn't finished . . . with one of us.

Bull and I stared into each others eyes while the unspoken question drifted above us like a dark storm cloud.

"Which one? . . ."

I thought about the big, gold eagle of an officer's hat and the gold bars on his shoulders. I remembered what Janie's uncle had said when I told him I was going to be an Officer. "At least we'll have one in the family. . . ."

"It's me, Bull," I said. "It's meant for me."

I felt his eyes on the back of my neck as Bull watched me walk down the long hallway to Rice's office. The heels of my boots made a hollow, empty sound with each step, a hopeless sound. The other guys in the class stood in the open doorways of their rooms and watched in silence as I passed.

The hallway seemed longer than it actually was. It seemed to grow in slow motion with each step. I felt the way a condemned man must feel as he walks "the last mile," passing the cells of the other prisoners on death row.

I didn't have to knock when I finally reached Rice's office. The door was open. He stood in front of his desk with his arms folded . . . waiting.

I saluted. Before I could say anything, he threw the key at me. It hit my chest and fell to the floor.

"Inspection in ten minutes!" he yelled.

I bent down and picked up the key.

"And, Yost," he said as I turned to leave, "You don't belong here."

I walked back to the room, unlocked the door and opened it.

"Holy shit! . . ." Bull gasped.

The room looked as if a madman had gone berserk. My bed had been turned upside down, its mattress thrown against the wall. Every drawer had been pulled from the dresser and its contents dumped.

We'd kept everything folded exactly the way the manual said. We never actually wore the T-shirts, underwear and socks. It was too hard to fold them again. The stuff in the dresser was for display, to pass inspection. We lived out of our footlockers. Now it was all ruined.

"Shit. . . ." Bull repeated as we stood looking through the doorway.

The floor had to be "spit shined" and so we never walked on it. If we did, it would smudge. Bull and I polished it every night and climbed on the furniture so that the shine wouldn't be messed. We hadn't stepped on the floor with our boots on in five months. The floor didn't matter now. Someone had ground a bar of soap in the middle of it. Bull's side of the room hadn't been touched.

"I'm sorry, Bull."

"It's O.K.," he said. . . . "I'll help you."

Bull grabbed one end of my bed and turned it back on its legs while I put the drawers in the dresser and started folding the clothes.

"We'll never be able to do this in ten minutes," I said.

We worked as quickly as we could, but it was impossible. I was still on the floor, folding a T-shirt when I saw Rice's boots in the doorway. I was sure that ten minutes hadn't passed. I yelled "Attention!" as he stepped into the room.

"Get out in the hall, Trumbauer."

Bull turned and walked out of the room.

"Heard from your Congressman lately?" Rice asked him sarcastically. Then he slammed the door and turned toward me.

"Yost . . . you are sorry," he said in that low, demeaning tone of his. The line had become meaningless from over-use. I stood at attention while he walked over to the dresser behind me. I heard the top drawer open slowly then slam shut. He opened the second drawer and slammed that one closed too.

I heard the third drawer open.

"ABOUT FACE!" he screamed in my left ear.

I turned. The drawer was open and he held socks in both hands.

"THESE AREN'T S.O.P., CANDIDATE!" he yelled as he threw them in my face. He turned back to the dresser, ripped out the drawer and dumped it. Then he threw the empty drawer against the wall and it fell to the floor with a loud crash.

Janie's picture looked at me from its frame on top of the dresser. I was proud of Janie. She was gorgeous and everybody said so. Even the Vietnamese who were going through the training with us had nodded their heads in approval when I put her picture on the dresser.

"Number One! . . ." "Movie Star! . . ." they'd said in their strange-sounding version of English.

Rice glanced at me. Then he picked up Janie's picture and held it in both hands, smudging the glass with his thumbs. I felt my jaw tighten and my hands clench themselves into fists.

He put the picture face up on the dresser. Then he found an ammo pouch and turned it inside-out. He took a pen knife from his pocket and like a fisherman gutting his catch, began scraping sand from the pouches seams.

When he had gathered all he could, he held the sand in his fist above Janie's picture. He looked into my eyes and slowly dumped it.

My finger nails dug deep into the palms of my hands. My face felt hot.

"YOU WANT TO HIT ME, DON'T YOU YOST? . . . DON'T YOU?!" GO ON, DO IT! . . . HIT ME! . . . DO IT! . . ." he shouted.

I wanted to break every bone. I wanted to tear the pock marked skin from his face. I pictured my fist smashing the thick lips and snapping the teeth. My knuckles itched. I felt the muscles around my eyes tighten as I glared at him.

I didn't actually say the words. I didn't have to say them. He heard them as clearly as if I had carved them deep into his forehead with his own pen knife.

"YOU WORTHLESS PIECE OF SHIT! I WON'T DO IT! . . . YOU SORRY BASTARD!"

Suddenly he backed away and like a lion tamer leaving a hungry animal's cage, he moved slowly toward the door and fumbled behind his back for the doorknob. Somehow, he managed to open it and backed out of the room.

A moment passed before my fists unclenched themselves. I picked up a T-shirt from the floor and used it to wipe the smudges and sand from Janie's picture.

I looked into her warm, brown eyes and felt my heart break.

"I'm sorry, Janie. . . ."

Chapter Twelve

"Thirty Days to Say Goodbye"

The light, Georgia rain blew softly against the window and formed itself into teardrops. One by one they trickled slowly down the windowpane and disappeared . . . a helpless procession being sacrificed to some vague, supposedly higher purpose.

Bull and the others had gone to Columbus on a twenty four hour pass. I stayed behind to cleanup the soap Lieutenant Rice had ground into the floor. I needed time to think.

It all seemed so hopeless as I scrubbed the floor on my hands and knees, listening to the rain.

If I dropped out, they'd send me to Vietnam. If I graduated, I'd go there anyway as a Platoon Leader and probably be killed. Even if I survived, I'd have to give the Army another year.

Graduation practice would begin tomorrow. In just a few more weeks, there would be a big parade. It was supposed to be a proud day, a proud moment to remember for the rest of your life. Names had already been posted for the "order of march," but my name wasn't on the list.

"It doesn't mean anything," Bull told me. "They just want even numbers so there won't be any stragglers. You know, so the class looks good when it marches past the reviewing stand. It doesn't mean you won't graduate. See, other guys' names are missing too . . ."

I didn't believe him. Bull was just being "Bull." It was why everybody liked him. It was his mission in life to make other people feel better.

I knew that if Rice had his way, I'd be "Re-cycled"; put back into another class and have to repeat two months of O.C.S. If that happened, I wouldn't be home on July 13th, our wedding day. There was no way I was going to put Janie through that.

I remembered the thirty-day leave. They always gave you a month before you went to Vietnam, didn't they? Didn't they always give you "Thirty days to say good-bye? . . ."

I pushed the bucket aside and went to the desk; pulled open the top drawer and found a calendar.

"If I drop out now . . ."

The date I'd circled on the calendar seemed to call out to me. July 13th was right in the middle of the thirty days.

I put the calendar away and went back to scrubbing the floor.

"Rice really did a job on this," I thought. "He really did it this time. . . ."

I felt her smiling down on me and I glanced up at Janie's picture on the dresser. It didn't matter to Janie if I was an officer or not. It really didn't matter to Janie. She didn't want me to join the Army in the first place.

As I worked all alone in the silence, trying to make things right again and knowing I couldn't, I remembered the Cinderella fairy tale. I leaned on the rag with both hands and pressed hard on the floor.

I guess part of growing up is letting go of fairy tales. It happens when the child inside of you stops believing. As the stubborn, green soap slowly disappeared from the floor, the Cinderella fairy tale of me and Janie in Germany disappeared with it. When it was gone, I put the bucket away and laid down on the bed, staring up at the ceiling. The floor still wasn't right but somehow I didn't care anymore. The decision had been made. All that was left was to call Janie and tell her.

Maybe it wasn't so bad. If you were married, they let your wife visit you after six months on R&R in Hawaii.

I looked at my watch. The class would be back soon. It was time. I got up from the bed and walked down the hallway to the dayroom. I stood there staring at the phone for what seemed to be an eternity before my hand suddenly grabbed the receiver.

"I want to make a person to person call to Clifton, New Jersey."

"I'm sorry," the operator said, "Could you please repeat that . . . a little more slowly?"

"I want to make a call to Clifton . . . Clifton, New Jersey, person to person . . . collect."

"May I have the name and number of the party?"

I gave the operator Janie's name and number and listened while the phone rang.

"Hello?"

I closed my eyes to savor the sound of her voice. It was like a cool drink of water, an oasis in the middle of a cruel, heartless desert.

"Will you accept a collect call from a Mr. Don Yost?"

"Yes! . . . Don! . . . Are you there?"

"Janie! . . ."

"I miss you so much!" she said.

"I miss you too. I really miss you. You have no idea how much. I'm sorry I wasn't at your graduation. How was it?"

"It was O.K. I guess, just a long ceremony. I wish you could've been there."

"I'm really sorry. . . ."

"It's all right. We took some pictures. . . ."

I could hear the disappointment in her voice. It wasn't "all right." There was nothing "all right" about any of this. I leaned against the wall and let a moment pass.

"Don, are you there?"

"Yeah . . .," I sighed, "I'm here."

"What's wrong?"

"Uh . . . nothing. . . . Nothing's wrong . . ."

"You don't sound right. . . ."

"Nothing's wrong. How are things going with the wedding?"

"It's really crazy around here. I got my gown, and we're going to the photographer next week."

I pictured her in a wedding gown, smiling as she walked down the aisle toward me . . . my Janie . . . I was so proud of her. . . .

"I'll bet it's beautiful," I said.

"I think you'll really like it. Everything's set for the honeymoon. We leave from New York on the 14th. I made reservations at the Deaville in Florida. Have you heard of it?"

"No, I never heard of it before. . . ."

"Well anyway, it looks nice from the brochure the travel agent gave me. It's right on the beach."

"It sounds great," I said.

It really sounded fantastic. I'd never stayed at a hotel before in my life. My first time on a plane was the flight to Georgia.

"There's still so much to do; I'll never get it all done. I wish you were here. I miss you so much. . . ."

"I'm sorry, Janie."

My voice sounded far away. It echoed back at me from the walls of the empty dayroom.

"What's the matter?" she asked. "I can tell something's wrong. . . ."

"It's just not . . . well, it's just not going the way I thought it would."

"You mean with the wedding?"

"No, not with the wedding. The wedding sounds perfect. You're doing a great job. I can't wait. . . ."

"Then what's the matter? You are going to be here aren't you?

"Sure, sure . . . I'll be there. Don't worry. . . ."

"Then what is it?"

I took a deep breath.

"Don . . . ?"

"I'm dropping out."

"What?"

"I'm dropping out of O.C.S."

"How come? . . . Why?"

"It's a long story.

"Well?"

"They're supposed to go easier on you after a while, but they're not letting up. If I don't drop out, I think I'll be 'Re-cycled.' "

Saying the words out loud embarrassed me.

"Re-cycled? What does 'Re-cycled' mean?"

"I won't graduate on time. It's like being left back. If that happens, I won't be there for the wedding, but . . ."

"Oh no!"

"Janie, wait a minute . . . That's why I'm dropping out, so I'll be home in time. I'll be there."

"Are you sure?"

"You know I wouldn't miss it. They give you a thirty day leave. We can be married and go on our honeymoon before I have to go."

"Before you have to go? Go where? . . ."

I pressed the palm of my hand against my forehead. It felt cold and damp. I felt like a nurse getting ready to stick a needle into a baby's arm. There was no easy way to do it.

"They don't like it if you drop out. . . ."

"What do you mean?"

"They punish you."

"Punish you? How?"

I took a deep breath and then exhaled the words.

"If you drop out, they send you to . . . Vietnam."

I said it as gently as I could. I tried to soften the words, I really tried but there was just no way to soften the sound of "Vietnam."

There was silence . . .

"Janie? Are you there? . . . Even if I graduated they'd still send me to Vietnam . . . Janie?"

I closed my eyes and felt all alone. I pressed the phone hard against my ear until it hurt. I could hear my pulse in the receiver.

"Janie, say something . . . please."

When she finally spoke, I could hear the hurt in her voice.

"I just can't believe you're telling me this. I thought they said you wouldn't go to Vietnam. What happened to all that stuff about living in Germany?"

I closed my eyes and felt my heart sink.

"It's not going to happen. They lied."

"They lied?"

"I'm not the only one they lied to. That's why half the class dropped out. Some guys are still writing to their Congressmen, trying to get out of it. Do you remember Chuck Pruit, the guy who went through Basic with me, the guy from Rutgers?"

"I think so," she said.

"Chuck dropped out right away. He's in Vietnam now."

Janie only knew Chuck by his name. I don't know why I thought it was so important to tell her that he dropped out "right away." I guess it made me feel better. I didn't quit "right away" like

Chuck. I'd made it through five months of O.C.S. I was almost a Senior Candidate. Rice hadn't been able to break me.

I was trying to salvage some sense of pride, some measure of dignity, but the fact that half the class had dropped out; that others had been lied to and that Chuck was in Vietnam didn't change a thing.

"So, we get married and then you go off right away to Vietnam?!"

"I'm sorry, Janie. . . ."

"Oh, Don. . . ."

It was only two words but all the failure, disappointment, guilt, heartache and fear were in them.

"Janie, there's not much I can do about it. . . ."

When she finally spoke, her voice was the whisper of someone who had just had her heart broken.

"What am I supposed to do while you're in Vietnam?"

"I don't know. Maybe you can teach school? It's only for a year."

"A year? . . . A whole year?!"

"Yeah, but after Vietnam, I'll be out of the Army. It'll all be over. If I was an officer I'd have to stay in for another year after that."

"You mean I won't see you for a whole year?!"

"In six months, we can spend a week in Hawaii . . ."

It was the only good thing I had to tell her. It sounded pathetic, absolutely pathetic. She didn't say anything.

"Did you hear what I said? They let me go to Hawaii for a week and you can meet me there."

"Is that supposed to make everything all right?"

"Janie, if I stay in and become an officer, I'll probably be killed over there."

"What?"

"They'll make me a Platoon Leader in the Infantry. A Platoon Leader's a target. That means they try to kill you first. Janie? . . . Are you there, Janie?"

"Don . . . I just don't know what to say."

"You sound like you're crying."

"I'll be all right."

I covered my eyes with the palm of my hand and felt sick. The realization came over me slowly. I'd go Vietnam and might even be killed there. But it was my mistake and I would have to face it. What had never really hit me before was that Janie would suffer through it too. She would have her own Vietnam, one custom-made to break her heart in a million ways. The loneliness and the fear would be the same. Maybe it would even be worse and it was all my fault.

"I'm sorry, Janie. I didn't want to put you through this. I didn't want it to turn out like this."

"Just come home," she said. "I miss you so much."

I felt embarrassed by the gentleness in her voice.

"I'll be there in a couple of weeks, around the first of July."

"I love you so much," she said.

I felt something warm trickle slowly down my cheek and I swallowed hard.

"I love you too, Janie."

I waited for the dial tone and listened to its dull hum for a moment. It sounded like a heart monitoring machine after the heart stops beating, when the patient has died. I hung up the phone and clicked off the monitor.

I thought there would be some sense of relief, but there were only feelings of failure and guilt as I slowly walked down the hallway back to the room.

Halfway down the hallway the guilt and failure turned to anger and bitterness, a bitterness I hadn't experienced before.

"So this is what Vietnam is like," I thought. "Just one personal heartbreak after another where innocent people get hurt and no-one cares."

I knew no-one would respect me for going to Vietnam, in fact they'd look down on me.

"Stupid enough to go to Vietnam," they'd say.

It wasn't right. The suffering Janie and I would go through at least deserved some respect didn't it? Was respect too much to ask?

It was still raining when I reached the doorway of the room. I went to the window and watched the endless procession of raindrops.

I placed the palm of my hand against the cold windowpane, and as I watched each helpless teardrop disappear, somehow I respected its sacrifice.

Chapter Thirteen

"A Quiet Kind of Heartbreak"

The Herald News, Monday, July 15, 1968

The marriage of Miss Jane Arlene Stolarski, Daughter of Mr. and Mrs. Benjamin Stolarski, 34 Mac Donald St. Clifton, and Pfc. Donald J. Yost, USA, son of Mr. and Mrs. Donald H. Yost, 5 Roseland Ave., Totowa, took place Saturday afternoon in Holy Rosary R.C. Church, Passaic. The bride's cousin, the Rev. Ronald R. Regula of St. Joseph R.C. Church, West Orange, celebrated the nuptial Mass. A reception followed at the Mountainside Inn, Clifton. The bride was gowned in silk organza appliqued with Alencon lace. Her veil was held by a seed pearl pillbox and she carried white roses and stephanotis. Her sister, Mrs. Henry F. Ryder, was matron of honor in a yellow A-line gown and carried carnations. Similarly attired were the bride's cousin, Mrs. Jay R. Hicks, and the groom's sisters, Christine and Theresa, who were bridesmaids. Two other sisters, Patricia and Lorraine, were junior bridesmaids. Mr. Ryder was best man. Chester Stolarski Jr., the bride's cousin, and James and Francis Yost, brothers of the groom, ushered. The bride's nephews, Kevin and Brian Ryder, were ring bearers.

Mrs. Yost received a B.S. degree in elementary education from Seton Hall University in June. Her husband, also an alumnus of Seton Hall, will begin a tour of duty in Vietnam at the end of the month.

They are honeymooning in Miami Beach.

Janie was beautiful in her wedding gown. I touched her cheek in the picture before I folded the newspaper article and put it back inside the shirt pocket of my jungle fatigues.

It seemed a lifetime had passed since I'd left her at Newark Airport five days ago. My mother and father had driven us there. We tried to find something to say but there was nothing to say except "Goodbye."

I remembered the World War II newsreels I'd seen of heroes going to war. People were cheering and bands were playing. Smiling faces leaned from windows to throw tickertape. Lovers embraced and soldiers waved from the train. There was something glorious and even noble about it. But there was nothing glorious or noble about going to Vietnam. It was private, like a funeral . . . a quiet kind of heartbreak.

My father shook my hand when it was time to go.

"Keep your head down, son. . . ."

"I will, Dad."

"Goodbye . . . Donnie . . ." my mother said. Her eyes began to fill as she hugged me.

"Don't worry, Mother. . . . I'll be allright . . ."

I turned toward Janie. Her pretty brown eyes were filled with tears. They overflowed and trickled slowly down her cheeks as she wrapped her arms around me. She buried her face against my shoulder and I could feel her whole body trembling.

"I miss you already," I whispered. "I'll write every day. . . . I promise . . . every day. . . ."

"Me too," she said.

"I love you, Janie."

She looked up at me. "I love you too."

Then she kissed me and I felt my heart break. I held her as long as I could, but now it was time to leave.

I looked back as I boarded the plane and Janie waved goodbye. The heartache and guilt I felt at that moment would stay with me. . . . I would feel it every day.

The flight from Newark to Washington State had been long and lonely. . . . I've never felt so lonely. After four days in Washington, they put me on a plane headed for Guam. One day later, the final stage of the journey had begun.

We would be there soon. I could sense it in the sound of the plane's engines. It all seemed so unreal; like it couldn't possibly be happening . . . a distorted daydream.

I thought they'd send us to Vietnam in a military plane but this was a Tiger Airlines passenger jet with Asian stewardesses. It was bizzare.

"Why do we need stewardesses?" I thought.

I envisioned some fat politician in Washington making the decision.

"And let's not forget the stewardesses," he must have said. "We want our boys to feel like their going on vacation. . . ."

He should have saved the money. We knew where we were going.

When the pilot's voice came over the speaker system he sounded bored — like he had made the trip once too often.

"This is your Captain," he mumbled in a foreign accent. "We will be in Cam Rahn in twenty minutes. . . . Temperature is one hundred and three. Humidity, ninety-two."

A few moments later, the seat belt warning and "No Smoking" signs flashed. The plane banked hard to the left and I strained against the seatbelt to see what I could from the window.

The South China Sea glistened like an emerald in the sun. Vietnam was lush and green. It didn't look like there was a war going on down there. The plane shook suddenly.

"What was that?!"

It was the first time the kid sitting next to me spoke. We hadn't said a word since we'd left Guam. He was scared.

"It's nothing," I said. "Just the landing gear going down."

"Are you sure?"

"Yeah, I'm sure. Don't worry about it."

"You sure we're not hit?"

"They can't reach us up here. We're still too high."

The roar of its engines caught up with the plane as it touched down and slowed to a stop. A minute later, the door opened and a Sergeant came on board.

"Welcome to the 'Nam," he said. "Follow me to the holding area."

The heat hit me like a furnace blast as I stepped through the door of the plane. I pulled the peak of the green fatigue cap down low to shield my eyes.

Cam Rahn Bay was a bustling city of steel quanset huts shrouded in a veil of dust. It was hard to breathe the heavy air. It had a sour, mildew smell to it, like vegetables left rotting in a garbage can.

Trucks belched blue smoke that smelled of diesel fuel and Huey helicopters landed and took off a moment later like bees pollinating flowers. Massive-52 bombers crouched in rows . . . waiting, their awesome, black bodies looking too big to fly, the tips of their huge wings nearly touching the ground.

The wind from Chinook cargo helicopters blew dirt high into the air. It settled on green plastic bags that were arranged in rows on the asphalt.

It was odd, the way they were lined up like that . . . like they were waiting for something. A kid standing next to me nudged me with his elbow.

"Are those . . . bodybags?" he asked in a low voice.

There must have been thirty of them, lying there in the heat . . . covered in dust . . . waiting patiently to go home. Their name tags seemed to come alive and dance in the helicopters' wind. It was an angry dance . . . a dance of defiance.

"Man . . . ," he said, "Those zippers must really be air-tight; with this heat and all. . . ."

"Yeah . . . air-tight . . .," I mumbled to myself.

The holding area was at the end of the row of bodybags. It was made of metal loading platforms anchored to the ground.

"Wait here for the buses," the sergeant said. "It won't be long."

We sat on our duffle bags and waited like newly arrived cargo. An hour passed before the four school buses pulled up. They were painted a dull green and their windows were covered with heavy wire mesh. Guys in faded jungle fatigues peered out at us through the wire like prisoners. When the doors opened, they filed past us in slow motion.

I didn't want to stare at them. They looked like they resented it, but it was hard not to stare. They seemed weary and old and there was bitterness in their eyes. They were going home but there was no joy or even happiness in their faces. I wondered what they'd been through to make them so old, so bitter.

"Three-sixty-five and a wake-up, mother fucker!" one of them yelled at us as they passed by.

It was frightening, watching the pathetic procession . . . visions of the future. I didn't want to be like them. I promised I wouldn't change. No matter what happened, I wouldn't let Vietnam turn me into what they'd become.

"Xin-Loi, Bitch!" Another yelled over his shoulder as we started boarding the empty buses. I didn't know what the words meant, but I understood.

"What's this wire for, sergeant?" somebody asked. "Is this supposed to keep us from runnin' away or somethin'?"

"No," he said, "Where you gonna run? . . . It's to keep the gooks from throwing grenades through the window."

Five minutes later, we were sitting in tents waiting to be told where we were going. Somebody had a map with strange sounding names on it . . . Pleiku . . . Da Nang . . . Phu Bai . . . Chu Lai . . . Bien Hoa. Everybody hoped they'd be sent South to Saigon. We thought it would be safer there.

"I heard they really caught some shit up north during Tet," somebody said.

I looked closer at the map. It was divided into sections. The section farthest north was labeled "I Corps." Khe Sahn was there and a place I'd hear about years later called "Mai Lai."

It was early next morning before the orders came down. By sunrise I was sitting alone on a landing pad waiting for a helicopter. It would take me to Chu Lai, the operations base of something called the "Americal Division" in "I Corps."

I wondered if Lieutenant Rice had anything to do with my being sent there. It would be just like him to make sure I went to the worst part of Vietnam.

As I watched the sky for the chopper's silhouette and listened for the sound of its blades, I wondered what Janie was doing on the other side of the world. The longing I felt for her had become a constant, dull ache.

The chopper finally arrived and I climbed inside. It was the first time I'd flown in one and I was sure I'd fall out of its open doors as it bolted from the ground and leaned to the right. I gripped the canvas seat as tightly as I could, my fingers aching from the strain. The pilot must have been showing off. He flew as low as he could, barely missing treetops and then shot wildly up into the air. I felt my stomach drop. It must have been his usual welcome for guys who were "New in Country."

I felt sick by the time we reached Chu Lai. I waited for the chopper's blades to stop rotating before I let go of the seat and got off.

Chu Lai had the same dust and smell of Cam Rahn but the atmosphere was different. The screams of jet fighter planes on their way to drop napalm told me I was getting closer. . . .

As I looked around, I noticed someone who seemed vaguely familiar.

"Lieutenant Swann? Is that you?" I shouted.

I grabbed my dufflebag and hurried toward the figure that stood in front of the headquarters building.

It made me feel better to see someone I recognized, even if it was a guy who had been a Tach Officer just a few months ago in O.C.S.

But there was no reaction from Swann, and as I approached him, he began to walk away.

"Maybe he didn't hear me," I thought.

"Lieutenant Swann?"

I ran to catch up with him.

"Remember me?"

He didn't stop. I was walking next to him now.

"Remember me Sir? . . . Yost, from O.C.S.? . . . Did you just get here too, Sir? . . ."

He finally turned his head. I looked into his face and felt a chill run up my spine. He had aged ten years and there was a vacant look in his eyes . . . "the thousand-yard stare."

He looked through me like I wasn't there and said nothing. As I watched him walk away, I wished I hadn't recognized him.

Seeing what was left of Lieutenant Swann made me realize that Vietnam wasn't a team effort.

"So this is how it's going to be," I thought. "Every man for himself."

I'd arrived alone. If I was able to live through it, I would leave alone.

"Mark off the days on your calendar. Keep yourself alive for Three-Sixty-Five (365) and a wake-up. Nothing else matters. Just stay alive. . . . All the rest don't mean nothin'.."

It was a prescription for paranoia.

By 2:00 that afternoon, I was back on a helicopter to a fire base named "Bronco." It was the base of operations of the 11th Infantry Brigade near a village called "Duc Pho."

"Bronco" was a barren, dirt hill with tents and bunkers surrounded by barbed wire in the middle of nowhere. Only the sound of artillery being fired from the top of the hill told me it wasn't deserted. The 105 rounds whistled overhead toward some unseen enemy, their flight ending in a dull thud in the distance.

There was a hand painted sign over the door of the command bunker that read "Home of the Jungle Warriors." As I started toward it, a kid on crutches caught up with me. He wasn't wearing a shirt and his right foot was wrapped in dirty gauze.

"Get down to the supply bunker, A.S.A.P. . . . You've got to be on that re-supply chopper in ten minutes, . . ." he said.

"Where's the supply bunker?"

"Follow me."

The helicopter's engine started as I rushed after him. When we got inside the supply bunker, no-one said a word. They gave me a dusty rucksack and started handing me stuff: hand grenades, C-rations, a claymore mine, two canteens, a helmet with a torn camouflage cover, an M-16 and ammunition. When they were finished, the rucksack weighed seventy pounds.

I ran back to the chopper and climbed on board just as it rose from the ground.

Chapter Fourteen

"Don't Mean Nothin' "

Monday, September 9th, 1968

> My pretty wife,
>
> I miss you so much, Janie. I haven't gotten any mail for the past three days, so I hope some comes today.
>
> We made another combat assault yesterday. All we've been doing for the past week is burning villages. It's the most disgusting thing I've ever seen. All you could hear was women and kids crying. We took about 15 young guys as VC suspects because of their ages.
>
> The "big, brave Americans" walk into a village armed to the teeth and bully a lot of people. I wouldn't trust any Vietnamese, but they get treated pretty rough and it makes you feel really crummy, seeing a kid scared of you because you look like a barbarian with your rifle and all those bullets.
>
> The VC would probably treat them a lot worse, but somehow it doesn't seem to justify what we do to these people we're supposed to be helping.
>
> It's funny . . . I feel sorry for them and afraid of them at the same time. What a stinking situation. . . .

I put the un-finished letter back in my rucksack not knowing if I would mail it. Maybe Janie didn't need to know what was really happening here. . . . Maybe I shouldn't tell her. Maybe it would be better if nobody knew.

I hadn't had a shower, or even shaved for the past week. My back was covered with a rash that wouldn't stop itching and I smelled.

They'd made me an assistant machine gunner and I had to carry the gun's ammunition besides everything else. The bullets were draped over my shoulders and criss-crossed on my chest like a Mexican bandit.

We would "hump" all day through heavy jungle that at times was so thick, we had to crawl on our bellies to get through it. It was almost impossible to breath the heavy, damp air and I gagged on its mildew smell.

There on the jungle floor, ants and leaches crawled under my clothes and feasted themselves on my flesh as if they were attracted by the insect repellent. The razor-sharp elephant grass sliced easily through the flesh of my hands and the salty sweat stung like alcohol as it flowed into the infected cuts.

The jungle distorted the sun's rays, creating an eerie world of shadow puppets. They pitied us in silence as we crawled slowly past them in the heat.

"Saddle-up," somebody said.

"Where the fuck are we goin' now?"

"Who gives a fuck? . . . I'm short, man. . . . 89 and a wake-up."

"89? . . . That ain't short . . ."

"Shorter than you are, asshole."

"89 ain't short, . . . mother fucker. . . ."

I groaned and lifted the weight of the rucksack onto my shoulders while they argued.

There was a strange stillness that day as we walked across the rice paddies toward the village. In the distance were old women and kids wearing the familiar black pajamas and pointed coolie hats of Vietnamese peasants. Their backs were bent toward the sun as they tended the rice like countless generations had done before them.

It was all so peaceful . . . a picture from *National Geographic*. The rhythmic sound of our boots sloshing the water was almost hypnotic.

As we got closer, an old Mammasan stared at us. She put down her wooden rake and began walking slowly toward the village, like she was going to make tea for unexpected guests.

I saw the frightened expression on her face when she glanced back at me. I'd never get used to that look. Why were they afraid of us? We were here to help them. We were going to save them from the Viet Cong. They didn't have to be afraid. . . .

"BANG!"

The shot startled me. The old woman fell face down in the rice paddy and lay there in the water, not moving. My knees felt weak . . . the world stood still.

There was no expression on the face of the guy standing next to me. His M-16 was still raised to his shoulder. He'd killed her for no reason.

It didn't seem real. . . . I felt numb, detached from it, like I was watching a bad movie.

I looked back toward the Vietnamese. They continued working as if nothing had happened — like death was a routine experience for them, so common it had become meaningless. The sloshing of our boots sounded different now . . . oppressive . . . foreboding . . . a death knell.

When we reached the Vietnamese they ignored us, like we were invisible. I sat down on a rice paddy dike only a few feet from the body. "Doc," our eighteen-year-old medic walked over to her and reached for the straw hat. The string was still underneath her chin and when he lifted the hat, her face came up out of the rice paddy with it. He looked at her for a long moment before he let go, letting her face splash back in the water.

"One confirmed V.C.," he said to himself.

His voice had a weary, matter-of-fact sound to it like he'd done this before and had grown tired of it.

"How do you know she was a V.C.?" I asked him.

He turned toward me. There was a sad, disgusted look on his young face.

"What?"

"How do you know she was a V.C.?" I repeated.

He glanced back at the body.

"She's dead, isn't she?"

An hour dragged by before her family came for her. Everything was quiet as death except for their crying. They tried to lift the limp body out of the rice paddy, but they kept dropping it back into the water.

It was lunch time. We opened our C rations and ate lima beans and ham while we watched them struggle. It was like eating popcorn at a horror movie.

The straw hat came off and I saw a small hole in the side of her head. There wasn't much blood . . . a "clean" kill.

After they'd dragged her away, a little girl about eight years old with big brown eyes came back for the hat. She picked it up and stood there staring at us. Tears were running down her round cheeks.

I wished she would go away. Guilt has a way of being magnified when it's reflected in the eyes of a child. But she wouldn't go away. She stayed there watching us with those big, brown, accusing eyes.

After a minute or two, Doc walked over and knelt down next to her. He gently wiped her face with the palm of his hand and then he reached into his pack. He found some cookies his mom had sent him and handed them to her. The little girl took them from him and ran off toward the village.

Doc knelt there for a long time. His back was toward me and I couldn't see his face but he looked like he was praying, kneeling there in the rice paddy mud with his head bowed.

My hand was shaking as I put another spoonful of lima beans and ham in my mouth. I couldn't swallow it and spit it out.

Moments later we were walking along a beach on the edge of the village. The sun reflected on the emerald surface of the South China Sea. The grass huts looked like they had been there forever and the beach was lined with old, handmade fishing boats that must have been handed down from one generation to the next. I was sure the people who lived in the village needed them to survive.

"Listen up! . . ." somebody yelled, "We're supposed to burn the fuckin' boats . . ."

"Oh . . . shit," I said under my breath.

There was no way I was going to do it. This was bullshit. They'll have to force me to do it. They'll have to put a gun to my head. I sat on the bow of one of the boats while the others rummaged through their packs for Zippo lighters.

I looked up and saw an old Papasan hobbling slowly toward me across the sand. He wouldn't have been able to walk without the stick he used as a crutch and each step seemed to be painful for him.

His face was shaded by the coolie hat but I could see the deep age lines around his eyes that said they'd seen too much pain.

Three of the boats were already burning by the time he reached me. He took off the hat, held it in his hands and looked into my eyes.

"G.I. number one . . .," he said in a timid voice.

Another boat caught fire. It was amazing how easily they burned. . . .

The Papasan must have thought I was an officer. He dropped slowly to his knees and there at my feet, he gathered handfuls of sand. Then he bowed his head and lifted the sand up to me as an offering . . . like a priest lifting the chalice.

"G.I. . . . number one . . ." He repeated over and over until it sounded like a litany.

I looked down on him with an icy stare as he groveled at my feet. There was nothing I could do. I stood up and walked away as the others set fire to his boat.

I glanced back at him just before we started moving through the village. The sky was filled with thick, black smoke now and the old Papasan knelt there next to his boat watching it as it burned.

Only very old people and children were in the village. They began screaming as we herded them ahead of us like they were cattle.

Somebody set one of the grass huts on fire. Nobody told us to burn the village, but it was too late now. All the hootches were going up in flames.

"Hell must be like this . . .," I thought.

It seemed odd that there were no weapons or rice cachets in the village like there had been in the others we'd destroyed. The huts were empty except for plates of rice and sleeping mats. I looked through the open doorway of one of the hootches as I passed and saw an old man with only one leg lying on a cot. He looked into my eyes and smiled a hopeless smile.

I nodded back and walked away feeling sorry for him. A moment later I heard an explosion and felt the ground move under my feet.

"What the hell was that?!" I yelled at the guy coming up behind me.

"They fuckin' blew him away, man. . . ."

"What? . . ."

It was hard to hear him over the screams.

"That old gook without the leg . . . in that hootch back there. . . ."

"Yeah? . . . What about him?"

"He couldn't walk."

"Yeah . . . so? . . ."

"So, they put a pound of C-4 under his cot and blew him the fuck away."

I closed my eyes and felt something die inside me.

"It don't mean nothin', man. . . ." he said as he clicked the Zippo lighter and set fire to another hootch. "It don't fuckin' mean nothin'. . . ."

Two days later, after the village was gone, we were on a hill getting ready to go out on night ambush.

Moe, our squad leader said he had something to tell us and there was a strange, troubled look on his face I'd never seen before.

"What's the matter, Moe?" Lefeaver asked him.

"That village we took out the other day . . ."

"Yeah, What about it?"

We gathered around him to hear what he was going to say.

"They made a fuckin' mistake . . ."

"What d'ya mean 'a mistake'? . . ."

"It was the wrong village . . ."

"What?!"

"Somthin' wrong with your ears?! We burned the wrong fuckin' village!"

Moe quickly turned and walked away, like he didn't want to deal with it.

No-one spoke. I looked around at the young faces. Their heads were bowed like high school kids who had just lost the biggest game of their lives and had no idea how to recover.

I went off by myself, away from the others. The sun was beginning to set over Vietnam and as I sat there all alone in the twilight, I cradled the M-16 in my arms and rocked slowly back and forth. There was a heavy, empty feeling somewhere deep down inside me.

"It don't mean nothin'. . . . It don't mean nothin'. . . ."

Saying the words didn't help. I thought about the old Mammasan lying face down in the rice paddy . . . how we ate C rations while her family carried her away and about the little girl with the big brown eyes.

I remembered how the old man had groveled at my feet, begging me not to burn his boat, and how I had stared back at him in cold silence . . . like a Nazi at the gas chamber.

I thought about the smile of the old Papasan they blew away just because he couldn't walk.

And as I sat there all alone in Vietnam's twilight, the screams of terrorized children echoed through my brain. Somehow I knew they would never go away.

Everything was different now. I was ashamed to be a part of it. The uniform I wore felt dirty against my skin and for the first time in my life, I felt ashamed to be an American.

I decided I wouldn't tell Janie. . . . I decided I'd never tell anyone.

Chapter Fifteen

"Goody's Last Day"

It lay on its side, a dead water buffalo bloating in the heat, its stiff legs sticking straight out like a huge, stuffed toy. Shrapnel had ripped the black skin from its side, exposing dark red flesh. It couldn't have been dead very long, a casualty of last night's artillery. I almost felt sorry for it as I walked past the body.

They told us the rockets that killed three guys on LZ Bronco the night before had come from the village up ahead. It looked quiet . . . deserted . . . guilty.

"Hey, Yost!" Goody shouted.

"Yeah?"

"Watch your step, man . . . punji stakes. . . . They're all over the place."

I was glad he was there. Goody was older than most of the others, maybe twenty-two or twenty-three. He'd been in the field for a long time and he knew what he was doing.

He had a blonde mustache and needed a shave. The red and white pack of Marlboros stuck in the band of his helmet looked out of place against the camouflage cover, and there was a Purple Heart pinned to the shoulder strap of his rucksack. It meant he only needed to be wounded one more time and they'd let him out of the field, give him an easy job back in the rear.

But Goody would be getting out soon anyway. He just got back from R&R with his wife and he was getting "short."

I took a few more steps before I saw them sticking up out of the ground: sticks of bamboo sharpened to a razor point. The V.C. surrounded their villages with them like barbed wire. The slightest scratch caused a deadly infection, and they were all around me like poisonous snakes ready to strike.

I didn't see it as much as I sensed it . . . something moving . . . there in the treeline twenty yards to my left.

I stood still, afraid to move. My face suddenly felt hot and I could hear the air as it rushed in and out of my nostrils. My grip tightened around the M-16 and its crisp "click" startled me as I flipped the selector switch to full automatic.

I turned slowly and knelt down on one knee, keeping my eyes on the treeline. It seemed closer now, its details distorted, magnified. A few seconds later, Goody, was kneeling next to me.

"What is it, man?" he asked in a low voice.

"There's something in there. . . ."

He suddenly burst out of the treeline and into the field in front of us, an old Papasan carrying a long, rusty sickle. His thin, white beard made him look like Father Time.

He wasn't expecting us to be there and stopped when he saw us, stunned.

A sense of relief washed over me and I felt Goody's hand on my shoulder.

"I'll cover you," he said.

I stood up and began walking slowly toward the old man. I was thirty feet away when he started running.

"HALT!"

He stopped and turned toward me. The expression on his face said he wanted to slice my head off.

"GET DOWN!"

He stood there staring at me, pretending not to understand. But I knew he understood. I felt the anger building inside me and pointed the rifle directly at his head.

"I SAID GET DOWN!"

I didn't recognize my voice. It sounded old and bitter. He slowly lowered his body to a squat but he held on to the sickle.

"DROP IT!"

He put it down without taking his eyes off me. I wanted him to be afraid but he didn't look scared at all, like it was routine to have a rifle aimed at his head.

He studied my face for a long moment. I thought I could do it if I had to . . . if he forced me to do it. But, somehow we both knew I wouldn't pull the trigger, and a toothless smile crossed his face.

"Number one . . . G.I.," he said.

Then he turned his head and shouted something toward the treeline.

One by one they came out of hiding. There must have been twenty little kids. The oldest couldn't have been more than eight.

They squatted on the ground behind the Papasan, making him look like a teacher on a field trip.

As they sat there watching me, I remembered the eyes of the little girl in the friendly village we'd destroyed a month ago. The sick feeling came back like it had happened only yesterday. I put the safety on and lowered the rifle.

"Oh man!" Goody laughed, "Looks like you captured the whole village . . . single handed!"

"What are we supposed to do now?" I asked him.

"I'll be damned if I know . . . guess you'll just have to adopt them!"

One of the little girls had tears in her eyes and she was cradling her arm.

"Hey Doc!" I shouted. "Come here a minute."

"What's the matter?"

"I think this little kid's hurt."

Doc knelt down beside her and gently brushed the hair away from her face.

"You number one Babysan," he said in a gentle voice. "Number one Babysan."

She smiled up at him.

The cut on her arm looked infected. The other kids watched as Doc gently cleaned the wound. He was always careful like that, especially when he took care of kids. He had a special place in his heart for them, and they knew it.

The "Babysan" watched him as he rummaged through his pack and found a bandage. Then he showed it to her.

"Number one," he said.

"Number one . . .," she repeated in a tiny voice.

When he finished bandaging her arm, Doc handed her one of the cookies his mom had sent him. The little girl stood up suddenly and wrapped her arms around his neck. Doc's face turned bright red and the kids giggled.

"Looks like love, Doc," Lefeaver said with a broad smile on his face as he and Moe walked over and sat down next to him.

Moe glanced at the kids.

"You got anymore of those cookies, Doc?"

"I think so . . . a few anyway."

Doc reached into his rucksack and handed Moe the plastic bag.

"I don't think there's enough."

"We've got enough. . . ." Lefeaver said as he pulled the ruck-sack off of his shoulders and opened it. "See, here's some of the cake Rita sent me, and . . ."

"Not that cake!" Moe yelled. "That's probably what killed the water buffalo back there!"

Lefeaver tried to be heard over the laughter. "It's good, man! . . . Well, anyway, she's just learnin' how to cook."

We all began digging through our rucksacks.

"I've got some stuff. . . ."

I looked up at the sound of Marshall's voice. He and Dave were walking toward us and Little John was following them.

Dave opened a can of C-rations and handed it to the Papasan. The old man nodded his head and started devouring whatever was in the can like he was starving.

"Oh, man!" Dave shouted. "He actually likes it!"

"What did you give him?" Little John asked.

"Lima beans and ham! . . . And he likes it!"

"He can have mine, too!" Marshall said, and threw another can over to him.

We found cookies and candy and tossed it to the kids. They scrambled after it like a flock of hungry birds and didn't leave a crumb.

"Hey, Yostie. . . . You been on R&R yet?"

I looked up at Goody. He was carrying the little girl with the bandaged arm and his Purple Heart was pinned to her shirt.

"Not yet."

"It's great, man . . . just like being back in the world."

I stood up and patted the little girl's head. She smiled shyly and buried her face in Goody's shoulder.

"I think she likes you . . ., Daddy."

Goody laughed.

"I'm practicing," he said. "I could be a daddy already . . . after R&R. . . ."

The smile on his face said he was remembering Hawaii.

"Hey, man . . . you got married just before you came over too, right?" he asked.

"Yeah . . . eighteen days before."

"Did you set up the allotment yet . . . for your wife I mean?"

"They're letting me go back on the supply chopper tonight to take care of it."

"Yeah," he said. "You'd better go. It's not a lot of money, but every little bit helps, right?"

"You've got that right."

Goody nodded and the little girl peeked over his shoulder at me as he turned and walked away.

A warm feeling came over me that day as I watched Doc and the others taking care of the kids. For that brief moment, there was no war in Vietnam.

I didn't know that it was the last day of Goody's life, and that I'd never see any of them again, except for Little John.

Two days later he'd be telling me about the 105 boobytrap that had blown them all away.

Chapter Sixteen

"The Shrapnel Inside"

The airport was deserted, its cold emptiness making us feel like we were the only two people left alive on the planet. R&R in Hawaii had been fantastic, too perfect to be real . . . a fairy tale with a heartbreak ending.

As Janie and I waited for the plane that would take me back to Vietnam, I learned that it's harder to say goodbye the second time. It would be five months before I could hold her again and I already missed her.

"Are you O.K.?"

"I guess so," she said. "Where's your ticket?"

"It's right here."

I took it out of my shirt pocket and showed it to her. She glanced at it for a moment and tears began to fill her pretty brown eyes.

"Five months will be over before you know it . . .," I said.

The words sounded pathetic. Five months would be an eternity.

"I'm sorry, Janie. . . ."

She suddenly buried her face against my shoulder and began to cry. "I don't want you to go," she whispered.

I felt a lump in my throat.

"Janie . . ."

She didn't deserve this. It was too much to ask. I closed my eyes and held her as tightly as I could. As we rocked slowly back and forth, a tear ran down my cheek and I brushed it away against my shoulder.

It was the first time I'd felt it: the bitterness burning deep in my gut. Like a dog that's been beaten too much and begins to turn mean.

I felt my jaw tighten. I remembered Lieutenant Rice in O.C.S. when he dumped the sand on her picture. I remembered calling her from Fort Benning to tell her I was going to Vietnam and how she'd cried.

I remembered how I missed her college graduation and how we'd spent Christmas apart. I realized we wouldn't be together on our first wedding anniversary, how that would be taken away from us too. Now Janie's heart was being broken again.

Her muffled sobs echoed from the airport's cold, gray walls and multiplied themselves. They took on a life of their own and surrounded us like a jeering crowd.

"Stupid enough to go to Vi-et-nam," they chanted. "Stupid enough to go to Vi-et-nam!"

The bitterness grew as I felt her trembling in my arms. And, for the first time in my life . . . I hated America.

I'd heard stories about guys who deserted while they were on R&R. They said they got on a plane and just kept going to Canada or Australia. I didn't have what it took to be a deserter. The stories said they always got caught anyway.

"At least I don't have to go back to the field," I said, trying to comfort her.

After I'd been wounded, I got a job as a reporter for the Brigade newspaper and only had go out in the field now when I needed to cover a story. But reminding Janie that I wasn't a "Grunt" anymore didn't help. We spent our last few moments holding each other, feeling the heaviness growing inside; the loneliness washing over us.

"It's time, Janie."

I felt like I was abandoning her as we walked slowly toward the door.

"Be careful . . .," she said.

"I will. . . . I love you."

"I love you too. . . ."

I brushed a tear from her cheek and Janie smiled. I was proud of her for being so brave. We kissed for the last time and I turned and walked through the door to the waiting plane.

I lowered myself into the seat, bowed my head and buried my face in my hands. I wanted so much to protect her from it, to make the nightmare go away. But I couldn't protect Janie from Vietnam. It was impossible . . . she loved me too much.

The next five months were the longest of my life. Writing about it forced me to see all the heartache, all the hypocrisy, all the suffering and all the sacrifice that America wanted to ignore.

I came home one week after a rock concert on a farm in upstate New York. They said the roads leading to "Woodstock" had been jammed. People had left their cars miles away and had to walk to the cornfield where the concert was being held.

They smoked pot and it rained. They had sex right there in the mud and there weren't enough toilets. It had been a "Lov In," the ultimate spring break . . . a young generation rebelling against the old values.

"Drop out." . . . "Tune in." . . . "Turn on." . . . "Free Lov."
America had gone insane.

No one spoke during the flight from Guam. Some of the guys had just gotten out of the field a few hours before and we were all exhausted. But a cheer went through the plane when the pilot's voice came over the intercom.

"We will be arriving in The United States of America in approximately ten minutes. . . . Welcome home!"

"Number One! . . . Number One!" we shouted as the plane banked to the left.

I looked out of the window as the plane descended through the clouds. There below us were the coastline and rolling hills of Washington State, covered with dark green pine trees. It was absolutely beautiful. I felt a warm feeling deep down inside me, like an immigrant seeing the Statue of Liberty for the first time.

I turned toward the kid sitting next to me. There was a broad smile on his face.

"Welcome home, man."

I thought it was over that day when the plane's wheels touched down. I didn't know that what would come to be know as "The Vietnam Experience" didn't even begin until you came home. . . . I didn't know America was ashamed of us.

The war and the protests against it were on the Six O'clock News every night. I tried to ignore it, but it bothered me when I saw the young Lieutenant on television being escorted down the court-house steps.

He was being court marshaled for what they called the "Mai Lai Massacre." The news reports said they'd forced women and children into a ditch and murdered them with machine guns.

"Innocent women and children," the reporter said. "Innocent women and children."

She repeated the line as if she couldn't believe it, as if she were shocked. I couldn't understand why she was shocked, why she couldn't believe it. Didn't she know what Vietnam was like? Didn't anyone know what was going on over there?

Lieutenant William Calley didn't look into the camera; he was trying to hide his face from it. But he couldn't hide the Division patch on his sleeve. It was the same as the one on my old uniform; the uniform I'd burried in the back of a closet.

I suddenly realized that I'd been there . . . walked through what used to be Mai Lai. I felt dirty and turned off the television. My uniform would stay safely hidden in the closet, my medals would stay buried in a dresser drawer.

The fall of Saigon in 1975 was the final perversion. The pictures of desperate people trying to grab the skids of the last heli-copter leaving the roof of the American Embassy somehow seemed appropriate. America's longest war, the only war America ever lost, was finally over. I didn't realize that fragments of Vietnam had logged themselves — like shrapnel — deep inside my brain . . . deep inside my heart.

It's possible to live with shrapnel inside you. You learn to ig-nore the dull ache after a while . . . learn to suppress it, force it back down . . . swallow the vomit.

It would remain there deep inside me, better left undisturbed.

Ten years later, the wounds began to fester, forcing the shrap-nel to the surface. . . .

Chapter Seventeen

"Welcome Home"

There was nothing very special about that Saturday in 1985. I might have had a little too much to drink, but I wasn't drunk. It was one of the kid's birthday parties. I was sitting at a picnic table with Harry and Jay in Harry's backyard talking, "Solving the world's problems," like guys do at family gatherings. Everyone else was in the house.

Harry was married to Janie's sister Arlene and had been Best Man at our wedding. He was an electrical engineer, a quiet, agreeable type. He reminded me of "Mr. Rogers," the guy on the kids' television show. I liked Harry, but we never talked about anything really important, just stuff about work, things like that. I can't remember Harry disagreeing with anything I ever said to him.

Jay had just finished telling one of his jokes about the Puerto Ricans in New York. He told it with a fake accent. He was good at telling jokes. He always had one about Puerto Ricans or Jews or blacks, and Jay always ran the conversation whenever the three of us were together.

He was big, an intimidating sales type. He was married to Janie's cousin Bernadette and I always thought of him as a brother-in-law. "He makes good money . . .," I remembered Janie's mother saying. It bothered me the way Harry nodded his head agreeing with everything Jay said.

Jay poured himself another gin and tonic and I guess we were beginning to feel a little mellow. It was time to get down to important things, big things . . . the truth. It usually happened after a few drinks. It was that time that always comes eventually when guys are sitting around drinking, you tell how you really feel about things . . . religion . . . the C.I.A. . . . who really killed John Kennedy? . . . values . . . The United States of America . . . life.

There was something in Jay's Puerto Rican Joke that for some reason reminded me of Moe . . . my squad leader in Vietnam . . . the guy who got his legs blown off by the 105.

I hadn't thought about Moe in a long time. I wondered how he was doing "Back in the world" with no legs. I poured more gin into my glass, probably too much gin.

"They're not all like that, Jay," I said.

"Who's not like that?"

There was a defensive tone in his voice, like I had challenged some deep belief of his. People didn't usually challenge Jay.

"Puerto Ricans. They're not all like that."

"They should send them all back where they came from with their '57 Chevies. . . ."

"You mean with the mud flaps and pompons?" Harry asked with a chuckle. He was trying to be as funny as Jay, but it wasn't working.

"Yeah, and with those dogs bobbing their heads in the back window."

Harry laughed and bobbed his head.

"You just don't know," I said. "I knew guys who were Puerto Rican. . . . They were good guys, too . . . really good guys."

"Oh, come on, will you? They're just like the niggers in Paterson. . . . They come over here and have a million kids and live on welfare and you and I pay for it."

Harry's head bobbed again and I took another sip of gin.

"They're not all like that, Jay."

"What makes you such an expert? Where'd you know Puerto Ricans anyway?"

"I was with them in Vietnam, and . . ."

Jay rolled his eyes. "Oh, not that again."

Harry chuckled.

I'd said the magic word. Just the mention of Vietnam always set people off. It was like that ever since I'd been home. It was why I'd stopped talking about it, why my medals were buried somewhere in a dresser drawer. I took another sip of gin.

Jay and Harry didn't know about the monster that lived inside me. I was home for just over a year when he appeared the first time. We were living in an apartment in Pennsylvania near Arlene and

Harry. It was my idea to move there. I thought Janie would be happy living close to her sister, but she said I'd forced her to move away from her parents out to the "boondocks." I didn't know how much I'd hurt her father by taking her to Pennsylvania. Our daughter Michele had just been born and Janie felt isolated with no-one to help her with the new baby.

We were arguing that day, fighting about something Arlene had said, something about me being different, that I'd changed since Vietnam.

"What does Arlene know about it!?" I yelled.

"She's only trying to help!" Janie shouted back. "You are different! Everybody says so!"

"I'm not any different!"

"You are! . . . You just can't see it!"

I hated hearing that people were talking about me behind my back, saying I was "different." I'd spent the whole year in Vietnam trying not to be changed by the insanity all around me. It had been the most desperate struggle of my life. If I was "different," then Vietnam had won after all. I suddenly felt an incredible anger.

"I'm not any different! Damnit! . . . I'm not different!"

I didn't even feel it when my fist hit the wall the first time.

"Damnit! . . . God Damnit!"

I must have hit the wall again. Michele started crying and Janie ran to the crib and picked her up.

"You're just like your father!"

My fist was still clenched when I looked toward her.

"Stay away from us!" she yelled. "Just stay away from us!"

Seeing her hold Michele close to her, as if she needed to protect her from me, made me even more angry.

"Damnit!" I yelled.

I hit the wall again and my fist smashed through the wallboard.

"Stop it! Just stop it!"

I felt a burning pain and looked down at my fist. The skin had been scraped from my knuckles and they were bleeding. It was strange how the hand didn't seem to be mine . . . like it belonged to someone else.

Beads of sweat formed on my forehead. I felt sick and suddenly afraid . . . really afraid, like the first moment after waking up from a horrible nightmare. I'd never been that scared, not even in Vietnam. This wasn't like my father. I'd never seen him do anything like this, not even when he'd been drinking.

I stood there holding the throbbing hand. The two people I loved most in the world were afraid of me and I felt ashamed.

I didn't know where he'd come from, this monster who flew into blind rages and hit walls until his knuckles bled. And yet, somehow I did know.

I swore I'd never let him out again. I built a bunker for him in my mind, a place where I could control him.

He would peer through the window and scowl at the world outside. He was bitter and always angry. He saw people as shallow and hypocritical, too concerned with the meaningless details of life. I had to watch him constantly. If I let my guard down, he'd break out of his bunker and "give somebody a little piece of Vietnam."

Jay poured himself another drink.

"I'm telling you, Jay, they were good guys."

I felt the monster stirring inside me. "There were a lot of black guys over there too, guys who got drafted."

"Well," Jay said, "That just shows you how dumb they are. I would have found some way out of it."

"Like you know so much . . .," I thought. The only military experience Jay had was being a cook in the peace-time Navy.

The monster started pounding on the wall of the bunker, demanding to be let out.

"What would you do?" I asked him. "Go to Canada? Be a draft dodger? Maybe even go to jail?"

"I don't know. But I sure as hell wouldn't have gone to Vietnam. I can tell you that."

Jay looked toward Harry, and when Harry nodded in agreement I felt betrayed.

"Do you remember when you first came back?" Jay asked, not really expecting me to answer.

"Harry, you won't believe this. Janie and Don came over to me and Bern's for dinner. I popped a champagne cork and Toastie here jumps under the table!"

Harry and Jay laughed like they were laughing at one of Jay's Puerto Rican jokes.

"Yeah, I guess that was pretty funny," I said, trying to be heard over their laughter. "But, I got over it. . . ."

The monster was disgusted. He always felt that way when I gave in to people.

They stopped laughing and Jay suddenly leaned across the table toward me, almost spilling his drink.

"I'd never let them send me into a war like that," he said. "That's for sure. Don't get me wrong. If it was for a good reason, if it was really to defend this country, I'd go, no question. But they'd better be marching up Main Street. . . . Then I'd kick their butts."

Harry nodded.

Jay was beginning to piss me off. He didn't know shit about it. He didn't know shit about anything and I was supposed to be impressed by how brave he would be if they were "Marching up Main Street"?

"You think that's what it's like? You think it's like some god damn John Wayne movie?!" It was my voice, but they were the monster's words.

"Hey, if somebody's shooting at me . . ."

"What if nobody's shooting at you, Jay? What if you had to kill women and kids? . . . Huh?! . . . What if you had to kill women and kids?"

I poured more gin and my hand was shaking.

"Why don't you just forget all that shit and get on with your life?"

Harry nodded.

It was an incredibly stupid question. I shook my head like a frustrated teacher.

"Because I can't forget it!" I said, mimicking his voice. "We were on a search and destroy mission once . . ."

Jay rolled his eyes and Harry's expression turned suddenly blank like he was watching a test pattern on television.

I didn't care if they wanted to hear my story or not. They didn't have to go to Vietnam, but they were going to hear about it. And if it made them uncomfortable, that was too damned bad. They could afford to be a little uncomfortable. They owed me that much.

"When we got to the village, they told us to burn the fishing boats that were on the beach. There was no way I was going to do it. . . . There was no way I was going to have any part of that shit."

There were blank stares on Harry and Jay's faces as I told the story. I'd seen that stare so often, I should have been used to it by now, but I'd never get used to it. It was like they were doing me some kind of favor, accommodating me . . . doing their bit for charity. I resented that blank stare; I resented it a lot.

"The women and kids started screaming. . . . It was awful. . . . I'll never forget their screaming. . . ."

I felt chills run up and down my spine. I always felt those chills when I remembered things from Vietnam. It didn't seem like they happened a long time ago. It was like they were still happening . . . I could see them happening now as I described them.

Jay put a cigarette in his mouth and fumbled through his shirt pockets for a light.

"Bern's been after me to quit," he said. Harry handed him the matches from the barbecue.

"This old guy was groveling at my feet. He had a lot of guts, coming up to me like that. He was lucky, someone else would have blown him away."

Harry leaned over and picked up a paper plate that had blown off the table, like it was so damn important . . . more important than what I was telling them.

"It's getting a little breezy out here," he said.

"They didn't tell us to take out the whole village, but some guys started burning hootches. . . ."

Jay looked at his Rolex and glanced at Harry. "Well, I'd better see if Bern's ready to go," he said and got up from the picnic bench. Harry went to the barbecue and started cleaning up.

I sat there for a long time staring into the bottom of my empty glass, still feeling the chills running up and down my spine.

"Welcome home. . . ." the monster said. Then he crept back inside his bunker.

"How much did you have to drink?!" Janie asked me as Michele and Dave got into the car to go home.

"Not that much; I'm O.K. to drive."

"Are you sure?"

"Yeah, I'm sure. . . . What's the matter?"

She didn't answer. She didn't say another word until after we were home and the kids were in bed.

"You did it to me again!" she said.

"What d'ya mean?"

"You embarrassed me in front of my family . . . again. Aren't you ever going to get over it? . . . You just had to bring it up didn't you? . . . You just had to bring up damn Vietnam!"

"I was just talking to Jay and Harry in the backyard . . ."

"Yeah . . ., and when Jay came into the house he told everybody you were crazy. He told everybody you needed help . . . 'a really sick pup', he said."

"What the hell does Jay know?! He doesn't know shit about it! He doesn't know shit about anything! . . . Nobody does! . . . Nobody!"

"If you need help you'd better get some," Janie said. "I've had it! I've just had it!"

What did they know, these people who'd never been there? What in the hell did they know? It was like I was trapped inside a bubble, looking out at the world . . . floating above it . . . lost somewhere between Vietnam and home.

It was like when I was a little kid, just three or four years old. We lived in Paterson on Walnut Street. One day I wandered out of the backyard and across the street to the park. Suddenly I had no idea where I was.

It was really scary, being lost. Everything seemed so big, so unfamiliar, so strange. The big people just looked down at me with blank stares and walked by, not saying anything.

There was a small submarine there. It was one of the first submarines ever invented. They'd fished it from the bottom of the Passaic river after it sunk and placed it on a concrete stand for everyone to see . . . a monument to somebody's broken dream. It towered over me. I sat down next to it, buried my face in my arms and started to cry.

I was all alone in a strange, frightening place . . . another planet. I heard a car's motor and looked up. It was my father's Oldsmobile. He had been driving through the park looking for me. He jumped out of the car and ran over to me.

"There you are, Donnie! . . . Everything's all right, son . . . It's all over now."

He picked me up and carried me to the car to take me home.

It was the way I'd felt ever since I'd been back . . . a little lost kid . . . needing to hear "It's all right, son. . . . It's all over, Donnie."

Chapter Eighteen

"Another Purple Heart"

He couldn't have been more than nineteen, dressed in jungle fatigues and holding an M-16 rifle. He was standing over the body of a dead gook and the look on his young face said he'd killed more than an enemy soldier . . . he'd killed part of himself too.

> "Studies have shown that
> at least fifty percent
> of all Vietnam Veterans
> who were in combat, suffer
> from some symptoms of Post
> Traumatic Stress Disorder."

The caption over the picture bothered me. It was too matter of fact . . . too definite . . . too final. I turned the page and looked into the sullen eyes of an older, bearded face. He was wearing a faded field jacket with a "First Cav" patch on the sleeve and he held a Purple Heart in his hand.

"Pathetic," I thought.

I'd seen pictures like this before on television. "Crazy Vietnam Veterans." . . . "Losers." . . . blaming their failed lives on Vietnam, using it as a handy excuse.

They couldn't hold down a job. They were drug addicts and alcoholics, scary time bombs that could go off at any moment and kill somebody.

They gathered at "The Wall" in Washington; drawn to it by some strange power like the lame drawn to Lourdes . . . like ghosts drawn to a graveyard. . . . They touched its cold granite and wept because their names weren't engraved there.

I'd seen it once. Janie and I stopped in Washington with Michele and Dave on our way back from a family vacation to Williamsburg.

So many names. . . . It seemed to go on forever.

I'd heard people say that seeing it almost made them cry. But I'd never heard anyone say they were embarrassed by it. I thought they should be embarrassed, maybe even ashamed.

A huge monument to the biggest mistake America has ever made. God, so many names . . . teenagers . . . only children. . . . And no one felt ashamed?

"Such a waste," I said as we stood there looking at it. "Pretty sad, huh? . . ."

"Do you want to look for somebody's name?" Janie asked.

"I only knew their nicknames. . . ."

Maybe I was supposed to feel like crying. Maybe I was supposed to touch it and wallow in Vietnam. Maybe I was supposed to hug one of the bearded derelicts who were dressed in old jungle fatigues and haunted the place. But I didn't feel like doing any of that.

I felt removed from it, like I was watching it on a movie screen, like it had nothing to do with me . . . the same way I'd felt in Vietnam.

"C'mon Janie, let's go."

"You ready?"

"Yeah. . . . Let's just go."

Didn't that prove there was nothing wrong with me? If it was still bothering me, I'd be running around dressed in Camo, feeling sorry for myself. I didn't even own a field jacket. I wore a tie to work.

And yet, I remembered thinking that day as we walked away from the Wall, "Maybe I should have felt something. . . ."

"The Veteran may experience vivid nightmares and flashbacks that force him to relive the traumatic experience."

"Flashbacks."

The printed word had a violent, out-of-control look to it. As the bearded face stared back at me from the page of the magazine, I could almost hear him yell like he was in a fire fight, thinking it was all happening again, thinking he was back there.

He crawled across his backyard on his belly, desperately trying to get away from some enemy no one else could see. Frightened neighbors peered out at him from behind curtained windows and shook their heads.

I'd never done anything as bizarre as that. And yet, sometimes, I guess every time a Huey flew overhead. . . .

I remembered that Saturday last August. I was cutting the grass in the backyard when my neighbor Bob Patterson called me.

"Hey, Don!"

I didn't hear him at first over the noise of the mower.

"Don! Look at this!"

"Oh, hi, Bob."

I shut off the mower and walked toward the fence. As I got closer, I saw he was holding a rifle.

Bob was a hunter. He took a week off from his computer job at Merk every deer season and rented a cabin in the Poconos.

"I bet this brings back memories," he said.

"An M-14?! . . . Where'd you get that?"

"Edelman's. It cost me a fortune."

"I wish I'd had one of these in Vietnam," I said as I took it from him. "At least it fires a man-stopping round; not like that M-16. That thing felt like a toy . . . always jamming-up."

I'd forgotten how heavy it was. I hadn't seen an M-14 since Basic Training. It felt substantial . . . it felt secure . . . like a weapon.

I checked to make sure it wasn't loaded. I wanted to impress Bob, let him see that I knew what I was doing. I knew he wouldn't be walking around with a loaded rifle. I raised it to my shoulder and aimed it at one of the trees in his yard.

It was subtle at first; almost a whimper.

"Whup . . . Whup . . ."

Nothing sounds quite like it . . . it has a heaviness to it, like the toll of a church bell on a rainy day, like the muffled drum of John Kennedy's funeral procession. It has the hopelessness of a lost child and the loneliness of the last leaf in Autumn. But nothing has its sadness. . . . There's nothing as sad as the sound of its rotors. . . . Nothing sounds like a Huey.

I glanced toward Bob. He was lighting a cigarette.

"Whup . . . Whup . . ."

I tried to ignore the sound. I peered through the rifle's sight again and felt my finger tighten on its trigger. A drop of sweat formed on my forehead and I wiped it against my shoulder.

"Whup . . . Whup . . . Whup . . ."

I pressed my cheek hard against the wooden stock and felt my hands tighten around it.

Chills began running up my spine.

"Whup . . . Whup . . . Whup . . . Whup . . ."

They were almost directly above us now.

"Weekend Warriors from Willow Grove," Bob shouted.

He was shielding his eyes from the sun and looking up at the sky.

"Whup . . . Whup . . . Whup . . . Whup . . ."

I glanced up at them . . . three Hueys in combat assault formation. The sound of their rotors made me swallow hard and I felt my jaw tighten.

I closed my eyes and bowed my head . . . like an altar boy at Benediction, made light-headed by the incense.

Suddenly, I felt it stinging my nostrils . . . the acrid smell of a smoke grenade . . . the ones we'd used in Vietnam to mark our position. . . .

"Whup . . . Whup . . . Whup . . . Whup . . ."

I felt the weight of the rucksack pressing down on my shoulders and the helmet liner digging into my forehead, the dirty fatigue jacket sticking against the sweat of my back. . . .

I felt the sting of the "Gook sores" that never healed and the open cuts on my hands from the elephant grass. . . .

I felt the heavy sadness that comes with the death of a friend and the guilt that comes on the screams of terrorized children. . . .

"Whup . . . Whup . . . Whup . . . Whup . . ."

And, most of all, I felt the loneliness . . . the gnawing heartache of being away from Janie. The constant longing for her had been the worst part of being in Vietnam.

"Whup . . . Whup . . . Whup . . . Whup . . ."

"Here, Bob!"

"Huh?"

"Take it back!"

"What?"

"The rifle!"

"What's the matter?"

"Nothin' . . . Nothin's the matter! . . . Just take it back!"

"You all right?"

I shook my head and shoved the rifle at him. We stood there watching the helicopters until they disappeared in the distance.

"You O.K.?" he asked when they were finally gone.

"Yeah . . ."

My knees were shaking and I felt drained; short of breath, like I'd just missed being hit by a Mack truck on the Turnpike.

"Maybe I'm still dealing with it . . ."

"Dealing with what?"

"Vietnam."

"That was a long time ago."

"Yeah, I know. But it doesn't go away. . . . It's like it happened yesterday."

"Maybe you should try to forget it."

There it was again . . . the stupid line I'd heard so many times before and could never understand.

How do you "try to forget"? It's impossible. Making the effort to forget brings it all back.

"I'm kind of sorry I missed it," Bob said.

I felt sorry for him. He had no idea what he was talking about.

I left him standing there, cradling the M-14 and went back to cutting the grass. I spent the rest of the day "trying to forget" Vietnam.

"I'm not crazy," I thought. "A Huey flies over and you remember Vietnam. What's so crazy about that?"

But as I turned the page of the magazine, I began to realize that there might be more to it than that. Remembering something is one thing, reliving it is something else.

I thought about that day when I hit the wall with my fist and that Saturday in Harry's backyard . . . how Jay told everybody I "needed help," and how I'd felt the monster stir inside me.

"Studies have shown that
Vietnam Veterans have most
in common with two other

groups: Rape Victims and
Holocaust Survivors . . ."

It scared me.

"Maybe I should talk to somebody. . . ." The thought made me wince like a drunk being told he's an alcoholic. If something was wrong with me, then I was like the bearded loser who's picture stared back at me from the magazine. I turned the page back to his picture.

"I'm not like you. . . . Damn it! . . . Crazy Vet!"

He looked back at me from the page with that blank, thousand-yard stare. He held the Purple Heart in the palm of his hand like he was offering it to me . . . like I needed another one.

And, suddenly, without really knowing why . . . I hated him.

Chapter Nineteen

"I Shouldn't Have Cried"

Dr. Sharon Daly didn't look like a Psychologist. She was thin, with long, blonde hair, and was dressed in a tan business suit. She must have been in her mid-thirties.

"A real woman of the '80s," I thought, as I sat in the leather chair in front of her mahogany desk. Somehow, I knew she drove a BMW to work.

There on her desk was a folder with my name on it, opened to the test I'd taken three years ago. It was a requirement at Eastman, Crowley, Betts & McCawley. They wouldn't hire anyone who didn't pass the day-long psychological tests. Even the people in the mail room had to take them. Most people didn't pass.

The tests talked about I.Q., energy level, sales and management ability. They could even tell if someone was alcoholic or on drugs or if they were having marriage problems. Some people refused to take them, said the stuff was too personal. Those people were never hired. It was assumed they had something to hide.

"Coffee?" Dr. Daly asked as she closed the door.

"No, thank you."

She nodded like no one ever said yes, sat down behind her desk and put on her glasses. They made her look older.

"I've reviewed your file," she said. "I see you've been promoted to Underwriting Manager?"

"That's right."

"Your tests show a slight temper, but it's good for a manager to have a temper, as long as it's controlled."

"I've never had a problem with it, especially not at work."

"Do you like being in management?" she asked.

"Yes, but — "

"I'm not surprised. Your tests show strong management characteristics. Have you ever considered sales?"

"Not really. . . . But that's not — "

I was about to tell her why I was there when her secretary's voice came over the intercom.

"Dr. Daly, I'm sorry to interrupt, but John Umberger of Westmark Corporation is on line two. He says it's very important."

"I'm sorry. Excuse me . . . I'll have to get this."

"That's alright," I said as she picked up the receiver.

"Hello, John. . . . I was about to call you. . . ."

I glanced down at my shoes. I'd spent some time polishing them the night before. They looked pretty good . . . professional.

"Yes, we've completed the testing. I'm sorry, but he's not recommended. The formal report isn't finished yet, but Dr. Burke said it will show poor interpersonal skills. I'm afraid we'll have to find someone else. . . . That's right . . . not recommended."

Dr. Daly leaned back against her executive chair, took off her glasses and looked up toward the ceiling.

"He has a "Y" management style, John. It won't fit the profile. . . . Yes, but references have to be taken with a grain of salt. . . . It doesn't matter. . . . The tests are never wrong.

"I'm with a client now. I'll have to get back to you. Maybe we should do lunch?"

She reached for her calendar.

"Thursday's open. . . . Bookbinder's? . . . Fine. I'll see you at twelve-thirty."

She hung up the phone and pushed the button on the intercom.

"Kathy?"

"Yes, Doctor?"

"Mark my schedule for lunch on Thursday with Westmark. And hold my calls for a few minutes please."

"Yes, Doctor."

"Where were we?" she asked.

"I'm not here about the tests, Doctor."

"Dr. Stein said you wanted to discuss career planning."

"Not really. . . . This isn't about work."

"What then?"

I reached into my suit coat pocket and took out the copy of the DISCOVER magazine article. It didn't seem appropriate now to actually show it to her . . . to mess up her expensive office with it. It would be like vomiting in church.

"I was in Vietnam."

The words hung in the air for a moment. Then they slowly floated down and came to rest on top of the immaculate desk.

"I read this article about some problems Vietnam vets are having . . . Dr. Stein said I could talk to you about it."

There was a confused look on Dr. Daly's face. "Dr. Stein told you to see me about this?"

"I don't think there's anything wrong with me. I just thought I'd ask about it."

"Did Dr. Stein mention that I'm not a clinical psychologist?"

"She said you might be able to refer me to someone. . . . If you really think it's necessary."

The annoyed look on her face said this wasn't in her job description. She had work to do. Westmark needed a middle manager, one who had acceptable "interpersonal skills," one who could pass the tests that were "never wrong."

"Well, all right . . . Is that the article?"

I nodded.

"May I see it?"

"I really don't think I've got a problem," I said as I leaned forward and handed it to her.

She put on her glasses and began scanning the article.

The plant standing in the corner needed water. Its drooping leaves were beginning to turn brown and I felt sorry for it.

"This is stupid," I thought. "She's not even a clinical psychologist. A waste of time, coming here." I glanced at my watch.

She finished looking at the article and handed it back like a rejected resume. I put it inside my jacket pocket, wishing I hadn't brought it with me, wishing I'd never come to see her. There was nothing wrong with me.

"Are you experiencing any symptoms?" she asked.

"I'm not anything like the guys they talk about in the magazine. I was only in the field for a few months before I got wounded. Then I got a job as a reporter.

"I probably didn't see enough to really get 'messed-up.' "

The words startled me. "Messed-up" was a phrase from Vietnam, part of the jargon. Nobody ever lost arms or legs there. Nobody ever got sucking chest wounds or shrapnel in the heart. They just got "messed-up."

I wondered if it meant anything; that I was talking like that again. I wanted to take the words back.

"Maybe if I tell you some of what happened there you can tell me if it was bad enough? You know, bad enough to mess me up?"

"Well, all right," she said. "But we haven't got much time."

"It won't take long."

I'd tell her a story that wouldn't mention any dying, one that wouldn't dirty her office.

"It was Easter Sunday and they sent me and a photographer, Lou Fedorski, out to the field to cover a story. There was a Chaplain out there saying Mass. . . ."

My tie suddenly felt tight around my neck and I loosened its knot.

"It was no big deal, just a human interest story. You know, about how guys were spending Easter in Vietnam? Propaganda, I guess."

Dr. Daly nodded like she knew something about propaganda and put my folder in her "Out" bin.

"The Mass was almost half over when we got off the Huey. The Chaplain was playing music on a portable tape recorder. . . . Johnny Cash."

Suddenly, I could hear it. I looked down at my hands. They were folded in my lap and they felt cold.

"Go on . . . ," Dr. Daly said.

"Do you know the song 'Were you there when they crucified my Lord?' "

"I think so. The old spiritual?"

A moment passed before I answered her.

"Yeah. Johnny Cash was singing it . . . on the Chaplain's tape recorder."

I felt chills run up my spine. The words floated inside my head:

"Were you there . . . when they
crucified . . . my Lord? . . .

"Were you there . . . when they
crucified . . . My Lord? . . ."

"There were about thirty guys sitting on the ground in a semi-circle around the altar. Well, it wasn't a real altar, just some ammo boxes . . . you know, like they'd make in the field to say Mass. . . ."

I glanced toward the plant in the corner of her office. It's leaves seemed to be drooping lower now. It was dying.

"Do you remember the line: 'Were you there when they hung Him on the tree'?"

Dr. Daly nodded.

"Well, there was a tree about thirty feet from where the Chaplain was saying Mass and there was this A.R.V.N."

"A what?"

"An A.R.V.N. soldier. That's what they called the Vietnamese who were with us, the ones who were supposed to be on our side. A.R.V.N. means Army of the Republic of Vietnam."

"He was wearing starched fatigues and his boots were spit-shined. It looked strange, starched fatigues out in the field. . . . God, he was mean looking. His helmet was pulled down low in front. . . . You could barely see his eyes . . . mean, black eyes. . . ."

I took a deep breath and shifted in the chair.

"Are you all right?"

I glanced toward the ceiling.

"Yeah, I guess so . . . ," I sighed. "Well, Johnny Cash was singing and there was this little kid . . ."

One of the brown leaves fell from the dying plant and drifted in slow motion down toward the beige rug. I closed my eyes and Johnny Cash's question echoed inside my head.

"Were you there when they
hung Him on the tree? . . ."

When I opened my eyes, the leaf had found its place on the rug. It lay there silently waiting to hear the story, as if it knew something about trees . . . as if it knew something about crucifixion. I stared at it while I told the story.

"He was just a little kid, couldn't have been more than eleven, maybe twelve . . . just a little kid. . . ."

My voice sounded different. It was cold, un-emotional, like I was reciting lines.

"They had his elbows tied together behind his back and the rope was pulled up over a tree limb. . . . The other end was tied around his ankles. . . . He was hanging there on the tree . . . like hunters hang dead deer.

The A.R.V.N. was interrogating him, jabbering something in Vietnamese, but the kid didn't say anything . . . didn't make a sound. . . ."

"*. . . sometimes it makes me*
tremble . . ."

"The A.R.V.N. cocked a '45 and shoved it into the kid's mouth. Fedorski started taking pictures of it, but they stopped him, told him not to take anymore pictures.

"The A.R.V.N. slammed the kid's body against the trunk of the tree. It made a dull thud. He did it again, but the kid just stared back at him . . . didn't say a word . . . not a word. . . . He just stared back into those eyes. . . .

"*When they cru-ci-fied. . . .*"

"The A.R.V.N. kept jabbering that high-pitched Vietnamese and slamming the kid's body against the tree . . . Johnny Cash kept singing."

I glanced toward the ceiling again, feeling like I was back there, feeling like I was watching it.

"The A.R.V.N. took a K-bar knife from his belt and he . . ."

I had to stop for a moment. Maybe she didn't need to hear this. . . . Maybe I should have picked a different story to tell her. . . .

"Well?" she said after a moment or two.

"He started to cut off the kid's ear."

The words laid there on the rug next to the dead leaf. I felt the bitterness, the deep anger growing inside me.

"The Priest could have done something. . . . He was a Captain. . . . He could have done something to stop it. . . .

"But he kept mumbling his prayers . . . just kept mumbling his prayers . . . and when he raised the chalice . . . I heard the kid moan."

The story was over, but the anger was still there. I glanced down at my shoes. The sick feeling was back in my gut and chills were running up my back.

"I don't know where God was."

When I looked up at Dr. Daly, there was a tear running down my cheek.

It surprised me. I'd never cried over that story before. "Don't mean nothin'," I'd told myself. . . . "Don't mean nothin.' "

I wiped the tear away with the back of my hand before she could see it. It embarrassed me.

She didn't say a word and there was that familiar blank stare on her face. I knew it had been a mistake to come here. She was one of those people who weren't there and couldn't understand.

I expected her to say that I wasn't crazy like the Vets who blamed everything on Vietnam and wanted people to feel sorry for them. I expected her to say there was nothing wrong with me, that any problem would have been picked up in her tests that were "never wrong."

Instead, she opened her desk drawer and found a business card.

"This is Dr. Mathias's card," she said. "His office is in Hanneman Hospital. . . . I think you'll like him."

"This can't be happening," I thought. "Why did I have to cry? . . . I never did that before. . . ."

"Do you really think I need to see him?" I asked.

She leaned toward me. "I wouldn't give you his card if I didn't think so."

It sounded like a verdict. I took the card from her like I was taking a speeding ticket from a cop. An hour later, when I got back to my office, there was a telephone message waiting for me:

"Dr. Mathias . . . Hanneman Hospital."

It was official now. I shouldn't have cried. . . .

Chapter Twenty

"Seven-Thirty?"

"She doesn't know what she's talking about," I thought as I began to dial the number. "She's not even a clinical psychologist."

"Five . . . Three . . . Nine . . ."

"Never even heard of P.T.S.D. . . . . Her glorious tests didn't show anything either . . . just a slight temper. . . . What does she know? . . . Big, fancy office, that's all. . . ."

"Eight . . . Six . . ."

I suddenly felt foolish and put the phone down.

"I shouldn't have cried . . . I should have never read that damn magazine article. . . ."

I lit my pipe and reached for the half-finished insurance application. I'd already wasted too much time. Reliance, Hartford, Aetna and Chubb were waiting.

Age of Building_____

Number of Stories_____

Occupancy_____

Contact for inspection_____

Has risk ever been declined?___Non-renewed?___

If "Yes," explain_____

The questions never changed. They just got more boring with age. I leaned back against my chair and watched the smoke from the pipe as it floated slowly toward the ceiling like a prayer.

One of the fluorescent lights was flickering. It felt tired . . . worn-out . . . weary . . . wounded. It was "hanging in," pretending there had been no power surges, trying to forget the electrical shocks the light switch on the wall had shot through it.

It must have known it wasn't like the other lights that shown brightly in arrogant rows on either side, but it wasn't ready to admit it was different, that it had been changed.

As it struggled, it made a low, buzzing sound, a murmur . . . whispering to itself so no one else could hear. "Don't mean nothin'," it said. "Don't mean nothin. . . ."

I closed the door to my office. Everybody noticed whenever I closed my office door. Maybe they thought I was doing their performance reviews. Maybe they thought I was looking for another job. Maybe I was just being paranoid.

I sat down behind the desk again and grabbed the phone before I could change my mind. It rang four or five times.

"He's not there. . . ."

I felt relieved and was about to hang up when he answered.

"Hello?"

"Dr. Mathias?"

"Yes. . . ."

I wondered why he had to answer the phone himself. Didn't this guy have a secretary?

"Doctor, this is Don Yost. Dr. Daly suggested I call you?"

"Yes. . . . Can you hold for a moment?"

"Sure."

I leaned back in my chair and closed my eyes.

"He doesn't even have a secretary. . . . What kind of a doctor doesn't have a secretary?"

A minute passed, then two. It seemed like an hour . . . lost in perpetual hold. I went back to the application and started answering the rest of its questions.

"Age of Building____?"

I didn't know and wrote "25 years" in the blank space. It was a safe answer. one that wouldn't be questioned. I had to get this finished and there were no buildings in Philadelphia less than 25 years old.

I looked up from my desk and glanced through the plexiglass window. Every office at Eastman, Crowley, Betts and McCawley had an inside window so they could see if you were working. They had a reputation for being a tough place to work, a "sweatshop," but they paid more than anyone else.

The Chairman of the Board, "J.B.," walked by. He paused outside my office and looked in at me, like a visitor at the zoo stopping to look at the monkeys.

His serious look made me nervous. He gestured like he was dialing a rotary phone and then pointed to himself, his way of telling me he wanted me to call him. I nodded that I understood and he walked away.

"He's probably wondering why the door is closed," I thought.

The Doctor's squeaky voice startled me when he finally got back on the phone.

"Thank you for holding. I've really been busy. . . ."

What made him think I wasn't busy? What made him think I could just sit there all day waiting for him to catch up on his paper work?

"That's O.K.," I lied.

The pipe had gone out and I leaned forward and tossed it into the ashtray.

"I want you to come in right away. As soon as possible."

There was a strange urgency in his voice and I resented it. I wondered what Dr. Daly must have told him to make him think he needed to see me "right away." She must have said I was a damned basket case or something. I wondered if she'd called J.B. too. Maybe that's what he wanted to talk to me about.

"Oh, shit . . .," I thought. "I hope she didn't tell J.B."

"Are you there?"

"Yes, Doctor, I'm still here."

"My schedule's really tight. I have to go Detroit on Friday for a seminar. I won't be able to see you for two weeks. Can you hang in?"

"Sure. There's no emergency."

"Can you wait until a week from Thursday?"

I felt someone looking in at me and when I glanced through the window again, J.B. was back. He was pointing at his watch. I nodded to let him know I'd seen him. He shook his head and walked away.

"Uh . . . yeah, a week from Thursday's fine."

"Are you sure?"

"Yeah, I'm sure."

"Can you wait that long?"

"Doctor, I've been waiting for sixteen years. I don't think two more weeks is going to make any difference."

"Are you sure?"

"Yeah, I'm sure. There's nothing wrong with me anyway."

"All right, then . . . a week from Thursday. But we'll have to make it for seven-thirty in the morning."

"Seven-thirty?"

"That's the only time I can see you. Do you know where my office is, Suite 712 Hanneman?"

"I guess I can find it."

"It's on the seventh floor. Wait for me in the hall if I'm late."

Somehow I had no doubt Dr. Mathias would be late.

"All right. I'll be there."

"If you need to talk to me before that, leave a message with my answering service."

"I'm sure I won't need to do that."

"I'll see you then."

The phone clicked and he was gone. I reached for my calendar and circled a week from next Thursday.

"Maybe I'll cancel."

I grabbed a pad, put on my suit jacket and headed for J.B.'s office, the big one in the corner. He was sitting behind his desk in his expensive suit. He never took off the pin-striped suit coat.

The President, Chet Powell, sat in the upholstered chair next to the sofa, smoking a cigarette. He was a chain smoker, short like J.B., with thick black hair that came down over his ears. His huge, square jaw made him look like a caveman and he leered at me through his aviator glasses as I stepped into the office.

"You wanted to see me, Jim?"

He nodded toward the straight-backed chair in front of his desk: the "hot seat."

"What's the status on Penn Corrugated?"

"It's out to market . . ."

"Did we go to A.I.G.?" Powell asked as he ground his cigarette in the ashtray.

"I've gone to Chubb, Reliance and . . ."

He didn't let me finish.

"We're down to sixty days and we haven't gone to A.I.G.?!"

"Well, yeah. But I can get the submission out there tomorrow, and . . ."

"That fuckin' market's going to be blocked!"

"I'll get it out there tomorrow. . . . I'll hand deliver it."

"Well, do it, goddamnit!"

"I will. . . . Anything else?"

"That's all Don," J.B. said. "Just make sure you take care of it. We don't want to lose A.I.G."

"Sure Jim. It'll be there tomorrow . . . first thing."

"Good," he said. "And Chet . . . I want to see you for a minute."

I felt angry as I drove home that day. The Schuylkill was backed-up with rush hour traffic and as I inched through it, I wondered what Janie would say when I told her I was going to see a psychologist . . . that maybe I was crazy. It wasn't bad enough that I had to go to Vietnam; not bad enough that she had to go through all of that too. Now I had to deal with this shit. Now I was crazy besides.

Some guy in a Mercedes cut in front of me and I felt my hands tighten on the wheel.

"You been to Vietnam sucker?! Huh? . . . You been to goddamn Vietnam?! . . . What in the hell do you know, huh?! . . . You don't know shit! . . . Damnit! . . . You don't know shit about anything!"

I knew the guy in the Mercedes couldn't hear me but it didn't matter. Yelling at him made me more angry. I wanted to hit something. I wanted to slam my fist through the goddamn windshield.

I glanced around at the other people stuck in the traffic. I was trapped; surrounded by "those people."

I turned the dial on the radio hard to the news station.

"KYW . . . News Radio . . . 1060 . . . News all the time . . . Tune in two, three, four times a day."

"Traffic One . . . Walt MacDonald reporting. . . . Delays westbound on the Schuylkill Expressway from Belmont to the Conshohocken curve."

"No shit."

I glanced out the car's window and saw the yellow helicopter flying above me. It wasn't exactly the sound of a Huey, but it was close enough. I felt like I was in a bunker again, peering out through its window.

When I reached the Conshohocken curve, I saw that the traffic jam was caused by a guy who had pulled off onto the shoulder to fix a flat tire.

"Oh . . . shit . . . is that all?" He wasn't blocking anything, but these stupid people just had to slow down to look at him. "Damn idiots."

It was an hour and ten minutes later when I finally got home. Janie and the kids had already finished eating dinner.

"What happened?" she asked as I walked through the front door.

"Nothing . . . just 'gaper block.' Some guy was fixing a flat and everybody was slowing down to watch him."

"I thought something happened to you. I tried to keep your supper warm."

"I'm sorry I'm late."

Michele and Dave were in the recreation room watching television and Janie poured another cup of coffee while I sat down to eat.

"So, what's new?" she asked.

"Not much. Do you remember I had to take those tests before I got my job? You know, those ink blot tests and all that stuff?"

"Yeah?"

"Well, I went to see that psychologist today."

"You did? . . . What for?"

"I don't know. . . . That magazine article."

"What article?"

"It was in that DISCOVER magazine. . . . You know, about Vietnam. I've figured I go in and ask them about it. But they didn't know much. . . ."

"How did you get out of work?"

"They let you go see them to talk about the tests. I went around lunchtime."

"Well, what did they say?"

"They're not what they call clincal psychologists. They just do testing. I don't think they knew anything about this stuff, but they gave me this guy's card."

I took Dr. Mathias's card out of my shirt pocket and handed it to her.

"I'm supposed to go see him a week from Thursday. His office is in Hanneman hospital."

"How are you going to do that?" Janie asked as she handed the card back.

"It's all right. The appointment is for seven-thirty in the morning. . . . I'll be back in time for work."

"Seven-thirty?! . . ."

"Yeah . . . he's busy. . . . It's the only time he can see me. . . . Can you pass me the milk?"

"You really think you need to see him?"

"I don't know. . . . It's no big deal."

Janie finished her coffee and started clearing the table.

"He'll probably say there's nothing wrong with me. . . . I just thought I'd ask him about it. That's all."

Janie didn't say anything, but I could feel that some of the pain was back again. I could see it in her eyes. I felt sorry for her and I wondered if Vietnam would ever leave us alone. . . .

Chapter Twenty-One

"Everybody Needs an Excuse"

The directory of Hanneman hospital is black and cold, hard as granite, like the Vietnam Veterans Memorial in Washington. I ran my finger over its listings until I found the word "Psychiatry." It seemed larger than the other words on the directory, hopeless and final . . . a name on a tombstone. Vietnam had left me here alone, abandoned in a hospital lobby, looking for the "Psychiatry" department of all things. It made me angry.

"I don't deserve this," I thought. "Not after Vietnam. . . . I don't deserve this."

Walking toward the elevator, I felt like I was back there again. I could almost smell it, could almost feel the heat . . . the wet fatigue jacket sticking against my back . . . the heavy, lonely feeling. . . . Maybe I was crazy after all.

The elevator slowly opened its door like it had grown weary of carrying life's casualties to the seventh floor. It waited impatiently for me to make up my mind.

I took a deep breath, stepped inside and watched my finger as it pressed number seven. Its door closed with a thud and the car began its assent into another world . . . a "Dust-off" taking me out of the field.

The "Medevac" set down a moment later. Its door slid open and I climbed off into an empty hallway.

I found his office and tried to turn the door knob, but it was locked. I glanced at my watch. It was exactly seven-thirty. Dr. Mathias would be late.

"What kind of a doctor doesn't have a receptionist?" I thought. "I'll give him fifteen minutes."

As I waited in the hallway, I looked out the window and down toward the parking lot. Hanneman was busy . . . so many sick people. I'd been lucky to get a parking space. The black attendant was already putting out the "Lot Full" sign.

"Seven dollars to park. . . . I wonder if any of this is covered."

It was close to eight-fifteen before a thin, bald man in his mid-forties walked down the hallway and stopped outside the office. He said nothing as he bent down to unlock the door . . . didn't even seem to know I was there . . . preoccupied.

"Dr. Mathias?"

"Yes?" he said, looking up at me over his glasses like I'd startled him.

"I'm Don Yost . . . We had a seven-thirty appointment?"

"An appointment?"

"At seven-thirty?"

"Oh, that's right. . . . Give me a minute to hang up my coat."

I remembered how urgent he'd made this sound on the phone. How could he have forgotten the appointment?

He opened the door and flicked on the light switch. The steel desk was buried under files and there were papers in stacks all over the place. He took a pile from an old chair and dropped it on the floor. Then he nodded for me to have a seat, took off his coat and hung it on a rack.

His plaid sport shirt with the sleeves rolled up past the elbows made him look like an auto mechanic ready to replace a muffler. I suddenly felt overdressed and loosened my tie.

The dingy office was incredibly small, no windows and no pictures on the drab, grey walls. . . . More a closet than an office . . . a confessional.

I expected him to say something about why he was late, maybe even apologize, but he didn't. It was almost eight-thirty. I couldn't be late for work and Vine Street would be jammed with rush-hour traffic by now.

"If this is a bad time for you, I can come back some other day."

"No. That won't be necessary," he said. "Tell me again why you're here."

"We had an appointment for seven-thirty . . . Dr. Daly referred me?"

"Oh, Dr. Daly . . . that's right."

He sat down behind his desk and began ruffling through the papers as if he was looking for lost notes; he gave up the search after a minute or two and leaned back against his chair.

"Someday I'll get organized," he said. "Why exactly did Dr. Daly suggest you see me?"

"I just wanted to know if I could have been affected by Vietnam. . . ."

The words sounded incredibly stupid bouncing off his office wall. How could I have not been affected by Vietnam?

"I read an article about Post Traumatic . . . something. You know . . . what Vietnam Vets have?"

"A magazine article?"

"It was in DISCOVER. . . ."

The smirk on his face made it obvious that he didn't put much faith in magazine articles . . . pop psychology written by amateurs . . . Freudian wannabees . . . Wayne Dyers without the degrees. I wondered if he even believed there was such a thing as "Post Traumatic . . . something."

"They said there's a good chance of having it if you were in combat, so I thought I'd ask about it. That's all."

Dr. Mathias took off his glasses, rubbed his eyes and shook his head like a school teacher who's just been asked the world's dumbest question. He put his glasses on again and folded his arms.

"Well," he said in a patronizing tone that made me feel like a little kid. "When were you in Vietnam?"

"Nineteen sixty-eight."

"Sixty-eight? That was a long time ago."

"I know."

He wrinkled a piece of paper and tossed it toward the overflowing waste basket. It missed. A moment passed before he spoke again.

"What did you do over there?"

"I was in the infantry for a while, and . . ."

"That's not what I asked you," he said. "What I mean is . . . Did you kill anybody?"

My neck suddenly felt hot and I unbuttoned my shirt collar. He tossed another wad of paper toward the basket and asked the question again.

"In Vietnam. . . . Did you kill anybody? . . . Women? . . . Kids?"

I guessed that was all he knew about it, that innocent women and kids were killed there. I wondered where he was in 1968.

"Well, did you?"

"No . . . I didn't kill anybody."

"You sure?"

"I saw people get killed, but I didn't do it. I did a lot of shooting, but it was at night at tree lines. We were getting hit. I don't think I killed anybody though, at least not that I know of."

Dr. Mathias stopped to think for a moment like he was trying to remember something he'd read in a medical journal. I could almost see him flipping through the pages in his mind. A long moment passed before he said the four words I wanted to hear.

"You don't have it."

I felt a weight come off of me like dropping a sixty-pound rucksack after humping it all day in the heat.

"What did you say?"

"Traumatic Stress. You don't have it."

"Oh, man . . . I thought so! I knew I was O.K. I wasn't in the field long enough to get messed-up. What did I say that told you I was O.K.?"

Dr. Mathias crushed another piece of paper into a ball and tossed it at the waste basket.

"You didn't kill anybody. . . ."

I watched the wad of paper as it hit the rim of the basket and fell to the floor next to the others.

"That's it? . . . You mean you can only get this stuff from killing people?"

He leaned forward across his cluttered desk, knocking his pen and pencil set to the floor. He left it there and narrowed his eyes. They were lifeless and dull behind his glasses . . . a plastic blue . . . the eyes of a mannequin.

"Then I'm O.K.?" I asked . . . "There's nothing wrong with me?"

"I didn't say that."

I was beginning to feel nervous, afraid of what he was going to say next . . . afraid he was going to tell me to pick up the rucksack again.

"Everybody needs an excuse," he said in a low voice. "Everybody needs an excuse to see a psychologist. . . ."

"An excuse?"

"That's right, an excuse."

He leaned back in his chair, folded his arms across his chest and peered over his glasses like a far-sighted high-school principal.

"Yours is as good as any other. There's even some sympathy attached to it. You know, war-related and all. People should feel sorry for you, right?"

"I don't need anybody feeling sorry for me. Nobody even wants to hear me talk about it, never mind feel sorry for me."

I picked up the pen and pencil set and put it back on his desk. A moment passed before he said anything.

"You'd like people to feel sorry for you, wouldn't you?"

"What for? I didn't see that much anyway. I was only in the field for six months when I got wounded. Then I got a job as a reporter. I don't need anybody feeling sorry for me."

"Wounded, too?"

"Yeah, so what? You answered my question. There's nothing wrong with me."

"I didn't say that."

"If I don't have Post Traumatic . . . whatever it is, then there's nothing wrong with me."

"You're here, aren't you? You took the trouble to come here, waited in the hall for more than forty minutes."

The words had a rehearsed, canned sound to them like he'd made this speech before.

"So?"

"So there's a problem. You wouldn't be here if there weren't a problem."

"What kind of problem?

"I don't know yet, but it's not about Vietnam. I'll need to see you once a week. Are Thursday's good for you?"

"I'm not so sure I need to come back. I don't think there's anything wrong with me. I just wanted to know if I've been affected by Vietnam and you say I haven't, so I'm O.K."

"I didn't say that," he said. "Now, how about Thursdays? It has to be at seven-thirty, though, I have other patients."

"I'm not so sure about this. . . ."

"You have to trust me. Now, how about Thursdays at seven-thirty?"

He reached for his "Week at a Glance" and took the pen from his shirt pocket. I rubbed my hand across my forehead. It felt damp and cold. I was tired. Sick and tired of all of it. A headache began throbbing in my left temple. Vine Street would be packed by now. I'd be late for work. I just needed to get out of his office.

"Well, it's as good as any other day," I heard myself say.

"All right then. I'll see you next week."

He marked the date in his appointment book like a used car salesman filling out an order form. Then he got up from behind his desk and opened the door to his office to tell me it was time to leave. . . . He had "other patients." I stopped as I passed him in the doorway.

"Doctor, are you sure there's something wrong with me?"

"It's like you're wearing a suit that's a size too small."

I had no idea what he meant.

"Trust me," he said.

But I didn't trust Dr. Mathias. I didn't think he knew anything about P.T.S.D. He'd probably never heard of it before, not until I'd mentioned it.

As I walked toward the parking lot, I realized he hadn't mentioned his fee. I'd get his bill for eighty-five dollars the following Monday.

I don't know why I went back. I guess it was because he was, after all a "clinical psychologist" and I'd been referred to him by Dr. Daly. "I wouldn't have given you his card if I didn't think you needed to see him," I remembered her saying. They had degrees, Doctorates in Psychology. They were supposed to know something about being crazy.

I tried to trust Dr. Mathias, but the next five weeks with him were a complete waste of time. We talked about my being the oldest of nine kids and about my father's drinking. We talked about pressure at work and we talked about me and Janie; but we never mentioned Vietnam again. We avoided it. Vietnam was just my excuse for seeing a psychologist and "everybody needs an excuse to see a psychologist . . ."

I called him on the Wednesday before the sixth session and told him I wouldn't be seeing him again. He agreed that I'd made remarkable progress with whatever was wrong with me.

"Be sure to call if you need me again," he said.

Somehow I think he knew I'd never call. His final bill came in the mail three days later.

I put Vietnam away, back where it belonged . . . in the bunker. I didn't talk about it and tried not to think about it, but I still felt angry and bitter. I knew the monster was still alive inside me.

I was rummaging through some papers in my breifcase a few months later and found the DISCOVER article buried under a pile of Chet Powell's inter-office memos.

As I read it again, I found something I hadn't paid much attention to before. It said something about "Vet Centers": free, store-front operations for Vietnam Vets . . . "A place to go to talk about it with someone who understands," it said. I needed to talk about it with somebody who could understand . . . somebody who'd been there. There was a list of offices and their phone numbers. One was on the corner of Broad and Olney. I could make it from my office in about fifteen minutes if I took Roosevelt Boulevard. I could go there during my lunch break if I hurried. . . .

Chapter Twenty-Two

"Hi, I'm Ellen"

"Hi, I'm Ellen."

I don't know what I was expecting to find at the "Vet Center," but whatever I expected, it wasn't "Ellen."

She was twenty-five or twenty-six; too young to know anything about Vietnam. Her long, black hair was pulled back away from her face and she was dressed in jeans, Reeboks and a baggy Duke sweatshirt.

"We've been expecting you."

"I thought everybody here was a Vietnam Vet. . . ." I blurted out without thinking.

She ignored the comment and turned toward a middle aged, black woman sitting behind a desk.

"Louise, would you get Don a cup of coffee please? I just made some. . . . It's fresh."

"I've got a form for you to fill out," Ellen said. "But it doesn't ask much — where you were in Vietnam, if you were in combat, stuff like that."

"Are you a psychologist, or something?" I asked as I took the form from her.

She smiled like the question was predictable.

"Yeah, something like that," she said, imitating the disbelief in my voice. "I've got a Masters in it."

"Where'd you go to school?"

"Temple, and Villanova for my Masters. You can sit here to fill this out. I'll be back in a minute, OK?."

"I guess so."

"Don't worry," she whispered as she touched my arm. "I promise not to bite."

Ellen disappeared into an office and I heard Louise chuckle to herself by the "Mr. Coffee" machine.

"It's black, I hope that's all right," she said when she brought the coffee. "We're all out of creamer."

"This'll be fine. Thank you."

She nodded, smiled again and went back to her paperwork. I sat down behind the desk Ellen had pointed to, loosened my tie and began filling out the form. It only took a minute. When I finished, I put the pen back in my suit coat pocket and waited.

A huge map of Vietnam hung on the wall behind Louise's desk with colored pins marking the headquarters of each Division. I hadn't seen a map with Duc Pho shown on it since Vietnam. It was odd how it made me feel comfortable and nervous at the same time, like I was visiting a cemetery.

The wall next to Ellen's office was covered in a field of military patches . . . "First Cav. . ." "Big Red One. . ." "Hundred and First Airborne." They looked like rows of tombstones. It took me a minute to find where the "Americal" was buried.

It wasn't flashy like the others; just a plain "Infantry" blue with white stars forming the Southern Cross constellation. I sat there staring at it like a mourner in a mausoleum . . . the most boring patch on the wall . . . the one most easily overlooked.

It seemed to be trying to hide there among the others, silent and guilty . . . a criminal caught in a "line-up," obvious in its attempt to be invisible.

It was at Mai Lai when they herded those women and kids into the ditch and blew them away.

It was on the Priest's sleeve as he celebrated the perversion of a Mass on Easter Sunday.

It was washed in Goody's blood when they hit the 105 and in Janie's tears as she pressed her face against my shoulder in Hawaii.

I was there when we burned the friendly village. And, looking at it now, I felt nothing.

"Finished?"

Ellen's voice startled me.

"Huh? Oh yeah, I guess so. . . . It was pretty easy."

"My office is over here."

Louise smiled up at me from her desk as I passed.

It was a small office with a single window and a metal chair next to the desk.

"Have a seat," Ellen said as she closed the door and plopped herself down in her chair; cross legged like an Indian. "We're pretty informal around here."

"I guess so. It's Ellen, right?"

She nodded.

"I thought there'd be Vietnam Vets here. How'd you get this job?"

"It wasn't easy. I really wanted it. I've been here a little over three years now."

"Do you like it?"

"Yeah. Guys are ready to talk about it now. It wasn't like that when I started. Nobody wanted to come to the Center in the beginning. Now they're coming out of the closet like you wouldn't believe. It can get pretty hairy sometimes. We got a call this morning from a guy who was having flashbacks. Dwight was able to get him on the phone and calm him down."

There was a worried expression on Ellen's face. She really cared about the Vet who was having "flashbacks."

Maybe she was only twenty-six and maybe she hadn't been in Vietnam. Maybe she didn't have a big, fancy office and a BMW like Dr. Daly or a "Doctorate in Clinical Psychology" like Dr. Mathias, but Ellen was different. She cared, and maybe that was enough.

"Who's Dwight?"

"My boss. He was in the Army; he served two tours in Vietnam . . . wounded twice."

"I'm sorry for asking all these questions," I said.

"That's O.K."

"It's just that I've been to a psychologist before and he didn't know anything about this stuff."

"I'm not surprised," Ellen said. "Some of them don't even think P.T.S.D. exists. That's why the VA set up these centers."

"You mean you work for the VA?"

"You wouldn't know it to look around this place would you?"

"Not at all."

"Well, we try."

"Is that why it's free, because it's the VA?"

"They mess up your mind and we help you fix it for free. Such a deal," she said in a fake Jewish accent.

"Yeah, 'Such a deal'," I repeated. "The guy I was going to charged me eighty-five bucks an hour."

"That's about right. What made you go see him?"

"They made me take some tests at work — ink blots, interviews with two psychologists, all that stuff. It was part of getting hired.

"I read a magazine article about problems Vietnam Vets were having, so I went back to the place where they did the testing. I figured they'd say there was nothing wrong with me. I told them a story about one of the things that happened over there and when I finished, I felt this tear running down my cheek.

"I never cried over anything that happened in Vietnam before and there I am in her fancy office with a tear running down my cheek, feeling stupid.

"Then she tells me she's not a clinical psychologist and gives me this guy's card; says I have to go see him, like it's a big emergency or something."

"What did he say?"

"He said the only way you get this stuff is if you killed somebody over there."

"What!? . . . He actually said that? . . . He told you you had to kill somebody!?"

"He asked if I'd killed any women or kids. When I told him I didn't kill anybody, he said Vietnam was just my excuse to see a psychologist; that I was looking for sympathy."

"That's bullshit! Half the guys coming in here were never in combat, never killed anybody!"

Ellen shook her head like she was disgusted.

"Well, that's what he said."

"How long were you in the field?"

"About six months. I was an assistant machine gunner with the American until I got wounded. Then I got a job as a reporter."

"Then you were in 'I Corps,' around Mai Lai?"

"Yeah. I walked through the place, but I didn't find out about the massacre until after I got home. I saw Calley on television. . . . I turned it off."

Ellen leaned forward in her chair.

"You saw some shit over there, didn't you?"

I didn't answer her right away. She was used to counseling "real" Vets, guys who were having flashbacks and nightmares, guys who were into drugs and alcohol, the ones who wore Camo and beards and haunted "The Wall" in Washington. I wasn't a "real" Vietnam Vet.

"I didn't see that much," I told her. "I wasn't in the field long enough. My squad got blown away, but I wasn't there when it happened. . . .

"We burned some villages; a lot of them. One turned out to be 'friendly.' Can you believe that? We burned a friendly village . . . kids afraid of us . . . screaming.

"I had an old man actually grovel at my feet, begging me not to burn his boat. He was kneeling in front of me . . . picking up handfuls of sand and letting it run through his fingers like a sacrifice or something. He must've thought I was an officer.

"They blew a Papasan away with a pound of C-4. He was missing a leg and he couldn't walk so they just blew him the hell away, like he was nothin'. . . . Just like he was nothin'. . . ."

Drops of sweat began forming on my forehead and I wiped them away with the sleeve of my suit coat. I'd never counted the things I'd seen in Vietnam before and listening to my monotone voice as it recited the litany surprised me. It was like I'd cut my face with a razor and didn't realize how deep the cut was until I saw the blood in the sink.

Maybe I had "seen some shit."

I felt sick and glanced out the window toward the SEPTA bus terminal on Olney Avenue. It had started raining and black faces were huddled under the green, fiberglass canopy trying to escape the storm.

It was somehow familiar . . . dark skinned faces in the rain, women and kids, huddled together for protection. . . .

I felt Ellen's hand on my shoulder and turned away from the window.

"Do you want to tell me the story? The one you told the psychologist?"

"Maybe this is all just a waste of time," I said. "I wasn't in the field long enough to get messed-up. . . ."

"I don't think it's a waste of time," Ellen said. "And besides, it's free; remember?"

"Well, I don't know. Maybe you can tell me what you think?"

"Sure."

"It was no big deal anyway. It happened when I was a reporter. It was on Easter Sunday . . ."

There was no emotion this time. My voice had a matter of fact tone to it. When I finished telling her the story, Ellen looked into my eyes for a long time without saying anything.

It was like she could see inside of me . . . deep into the bunker. Somehow I knew she saw the monster sulking there in the darkness and it embarrassed me.

"That's disgusting!" she said finally.

I felt a heavy weight lift off of me. Ellen understood. She thought the story was "disgusting" and she wasn't afraid to say so.

It was "disgusting" to watch a kid having his ear cut off while a Priest said Mass. It was "disgusting" to destroy a friendly village and kill innocent people. It was "disgusting" that Goody had to die for nothing and that Janie's heart had to be broken. Everything about Vietnam was "disgusting." Maybe I wasn't crazy after all. Maybe I was just "disgusted."

"Well, what do you think? Do I have this Vietnam stuff or not?"

"Tell me how you felt that Easter Sunday."

"You mean while it was happening?"

"Yeah . . . while it was happening."

"I didn't feel anything."

"You didn't feel anything while the A.R.V.N. was cutting off the little boy's ear?"

"I was just surprised that his fatigues were starched that's all. I couldn't understand where he got starched fatigues out there in the field. They looked really strange . . . you know, too pressed . . . too clean . . . too perfect . . . I couldn't understand how he . . . oh, man . . ."

"What's the matter?"

"All I felt was surprised that the A.R.V.N.'s fatigues were starched. . . . That's all I felt. . . ."

"That's not unusual."

"It's not?"

"It's like a circuit breaker goes off inside you when stuff like that happens. You know . . . a power surge and the circuit breaker trips? I hear it all the time. Guys see something really horrible and don't feel anything or they focus on some trivial thing."

"Like the A.R.V.N.'s starched fatigues?"

"Yeah, like the A.R.V.N.'s starched fatigues. It's part of the body's defense system. The emotions shut down. It helps you to survive."

"Is that why the little kid didn't say anything? He was numbed-out?"

"Probably. The circuit breaker tripped."

"That's really weird. I mean, I didn't feel anything. . . ."

"How do you think you should have felt?"

The question pissed me off.

"How do you think I should've felt, Ellen?! They were cutting off a kid's ear while a priest was saying Mass!"

"Every damn thing I believed in was shot to shit! Just another Easter Sunday in goddamn Vietnam, right?!

"So much for the 'Mom and apple pie' bullshit! So much for the United States of Goddamn America! Where in the hell was John Wayne, huh? Where in the hell was God?! How the hell do you think I should've felt?!"

My hands were clenched in fists and I suddenly realized I was sitting on the edge of the chair.

"I'm sorry," I said as I rubbed the back of my hand across my eyes and pushed myself back against the chair. "I didn't mean to yell at you like that."

I glanced out the window again toward the bus terminal. It was empty. The dark faces were gone now.

"If you could see that priest today," Ellen said, "what would you say to him?"

"I'd tell him he's a hypocrite and a coward, a bureaucratic asshole. I'd tell him that the Church I believed in my whole life is full of shit."

"Do you still go to church?"

"Yeah, every Sunday. But it's different now."

"How?"

"I go for Communion and to listen to the Gospel, but I don't listen to what the priests say. . . . They don't know shit. Are you Catholic by any chance?"

"Jewish."

"Well, maybe you don't know what I'm talking about then."

"I understand. You're really bitter, aren't you?"

"Yeah, I'm bitter. I was an altar boy until my freshman year in high school. I grew out of the Cassock and Surplus, had to wear the priest's outfit for the last year. . . . Got an "A" in Moral Theology at Seton Hall. A lot of good that did.

"Well, what do you think? . . . Do I have this stuff?"

"You've been through more shit than most of the guys who come through here," she said.

"I have?"

"Yeah, most of them were never in the field."

"But they've got problems, right — drugs, alcohol, stuff like that?"

"Some of them."

"They're unemployed on welfare right? . . . Beards, Camo?"

"Some."

"O.K. Ellen, how many guys do you have coming in here wearing ties, huh? . . . How many?!"

"Well, not that many. But you're a Vietnam Vet, aren't you?"

"Not me. . . . My body might have been there, but I'm no 'Vietnam Vet'!"

She let me sit there quietly for a moment so I could hear how stupid I sounded.

I remembered when the Sergeant told me to walk point across the field where my squad had been blown away the day before. I felt the same way now, sitting in Ellen's office. I needed to know how far I had to go, how long the journey would be.

"How bad is it?" I asked.

"On a scale of one to ten?"

I nodded.

"It's about a five. . . ."

"How can you be so sure?"

"There's no doubt about it," she said. "I can see it. It's in your eyes. . . ."

Chapter Twenty-Three

"Institutional Green Is Eternal"

I went back to see Ellen every Wednesday for the next twelve weeks to talk about things I'd seen in Vietnam and how I felt about them. It was like going back in time to dig up emotions I'd left in Southeast Asia eighteen years earlier. The feelings hadn't aged, they'd just been covered up, buried alive. . . .

"He was just an old man. He was lying on a cot and I could see he was missing a leg. I was only fifty or sixty feet away from him when I heard the explosion. A guy coming up behind me said they'd blown him away with a pound of C-4 because he couldn't walk. 'Don't mean nothin', I remember him saying . . . 'Don't mean nothin', man.'

"Well you know what, Ellen? . . . It did mean something. It mattered. . . . It mattered a lot."

"How did you feel?"

"Like this . . ."

I bowed my head and slumped down in the chair to show her how I'd felt that day. No words could express it and somehow, eighteen years later, I felt like it had happened only a moment ago.

"I guess I felt hollow . . . I guess I felt like part of me died . . .

"Do you know what it takes to do that to somebody, Ellen? First you've got to take the C-4 out of your rucksack and stick a percussion cap in it. . . . Then you've got to put it under the cot and run the wire back as far as you can and screw the end of it into the detonator. Then you have to lie down on the ground and you squeeze the handle three times . . ."

I pressed my hand hard against my temple like I was trying to get rid of a migraine. Ellen didn't say anything and after a minute or two, I rested my neck against the back of the chair and looked up toward the ceiling.

The paint had cracked and was starting to peel. The thin, white veneer was tired of clinging to the ceiling. It was beginning to fall away, exposing the true color: a drab, institutional green.

Institutional green doesn't fade. You can cover it and you can keep touching it up so you forget about it for a while, but it's always there. It stays hidden just beneath the surface and eventually it shows itself in bits and pieces. Institutional green is eternal. It looks exactly the same eighteen years later as it did the day the ceiling was first desecrated with it.

"Did I ever tell you my father lost his leg in World War II?"

"No."

"It happened in an apple orchard in France. He got hit by a mortar round. They took it off just below his left knee. He always said he was lucky they didn't cut it off above the knee. He couldn't wear an artificial leg if they cut it off above the knee. The old man's leg was off at the hip. . . ."

I lowered my head and rubbed my hand across my eyes.

"Do you want to say something to those guys?" Ellen asked.

"What?"

"Do you want to say something to them?"

"It was eighteen years ago, Ellen. . . ."

"I know, but I think there's something you need to tell them."

Maybe I needed to hear myself say it out loud. Maybe there'd be some satisfaction in it, like talking to a tombstone, believing the person buried beneath it is somehow able to hear.

"I guess there's something I'd like to tell them. . . ."

I felt the anger build in me as I straightened myself in the chair, leaned forward and looked into her eyes.

"I'll tell you what I'd like to do. . . ."

There was a cold, bitter tone to the voice that came from the bunker deep inside me. I spoke slowly, taking the time to pronounce every word clearly.

"I'd like to take the pound of C-4 and cram it up their asses. Then I'd blow the shit out of them and ask them: 'How does that feel, guys, huh?' . . . 'How does that feel?' . . . 'Don't Mean Nothin'.'

"Then I'd take the machine-gun and throw it to the Gooks; raise my hands in the air and tell them: "Do it, goddamn it; do it!"

I'd always felt ashamed when I remembered how they'd killed the old man. The sick, hollow feeling always came back whenever I thought about him. But now it was different. Now the emptiness was filled with rage and bitterness.

"That story really upsets you, doesn't it?" Ellen asked.

It was a dumb question, one that didn't need an answer.

"Do you know what really pisses me off?"

"What?"

"I don't understand what happened."

"What do you mean?"

"I did everything I was supposed to do my whole, stupid life and now I'm sitting here with you trying to figure out why in the hell I'm crazy. What happened, Ellen?

"All I did was go to Vietnam. What was I supposed to do? Go over the Peace Bridge to Canada? Burn my draft card and turn into some goddamn hippie? Whatever happened to serving your country, huh? Whatever happened to that pile of bullshit?

"And now I'm the one who's stupid for being there? Now I'm the one who's crazy? Well excuse the hell out of me . . ."

I reached into my shirt pocket for the pack of Marlboros I'd bought on the way to the center, tore it open and shook one out.

"I didn't know you smoke."

"Just a pipe. . . . Sometimes these are easier."

My hand was shaking as I lit the cigarette and tossed the smoking match into the ashtray on her desk.

"You feel guilty, don't you?"

"Why should I?"

She didn't answer.

"I didn't do anything, Ellen. I didn't even burn any hootches that day. . . ."

I took a hard puff on the cigarette. The smoke had the pungent, familiar smell of burning straw.

"Then why do you feel guilty? You just said you'd tell them to kill you, didn't you?"

"Yeah, but I didn't do anything."

"Then why?"

"Just being there was enough. Just being part of it. . . . It was like being a goddamn Nazi at the gas chamber."

I leaned forward and crushed the half burned cigarette in the ashtray.

"Could you have done anything to stop it?"

"No way. . . . It was a war, remember?"

"And war sucks, doesn't it?"

"Yeah, war sucks. . . . No shit."

"Was this the same day the friendly village was burned?"

"Yeah."

"Tell me about it."

"What is this, some kind of exorcism?"

"Tell me what happened that day."

I lit another cigarette and Ellen pushed the ashtray closer to the edge of her desk. I watched the smoke as it drifted slowly toward the ceiling like incense.

"We were walking toward the village through a rice paddy. An M-16 went off and I saw the Mamasan fall face down in the water."

"Where did the shot come from?"

"Next to me. The guy on my left shot her. When I looked at him he was still aiming through the sight of the rifle. She wasn't doing anything. He shot her in the head for no reason . . . guess he was bored."

"Tell me about him."

"What do you want to know? He had a round, ugly face and he needed a shave. He was a truck driver back in the world. Now he was an asshole with an M-16.

"Go on. . . ."

"There was no expression on his face. I can still see the dumb stare, like a deer caught in the headlights, you know? What an ass . . ."

"Are you sure he shot her for no reason?"

"Yeah, I'm sure."

"Think about it for a minute."

I took another puff on the cigarette while I thought about the guy I'd hated for eighteen years.

"He shot her for no reason . . . that's all . . . no goddamn reason at all."

"Why did he single her out from the others?"

"I guess because she started walking toward the village."

"Was she walking or running?"

"All right, I guess she was running."

"Weren't you supposed to shoot anybody who ran? Didn't that mean they were V.C.?"

"Yeah, but we were in the wrong village. She wasn't a V.C. so he killed her for nothing."

"But he didn't know that when he shot her, did he? . . . She knew she wasn't supposed to move, right?"

"Yeah, she knew. They all knew."

"How did he act after it happened?"

"I told you, there was no expression on his face."

"Did he say anything?"

"No."

"Did he go over to look at the body?"

"He got as far away from it as he could, went off by himself. It was like the world stopped; everything got so quiet."

"How do you think he felt?"

I'd never thought about how he'd felt. Now it seemed important.

"I guess he felt bad about it. Maybe he didn't feel anything. . . . I don't know."

"What did you do?"

"I just kept walking 'till I got up next to her. Then I sat down on a rice paddy dike."

"What happened then?"

"Her family came to get her. They couldn't even pick her up the right way, kept dropping her back into the water. There was a little girl with big, brown eyes. I guess the old woman was her grandmother."

"How did you feel?"

"I can't remember."

"There must have been something."

"I told you, I can't remember."

It was frustrating; trying to conjure up whatever emotion must have been there eighteen years ago. It was like trying to remember the details of a nightmare. Not being able to remember how I'd felt scared me.

"I can't remember anything, Ellen. I can't remember anything except . . ."

"What?"

"The lima beans and ham were greasy."

"What are you talking about?"

"The lima beans and ham . . . they were greasy. I opened a can of C rations and ate it while I watched them."

"You mean you were having lunch?"

"Yeah . . . but I couldn't swallow it. I put it in my mouth, but I couldn't swallow it. . . . That means something, doesn't it?"

"What do you think it means?"

"It must have bothered me. At least I wasn't like the guy who shot her, right?"

Ellen didn't say anything. She just sat there staring at me. I'd always thought not being able to swallow the C rations meant I was better than the guy who'd shot the old woman. It gave me the right to hate him. Now I wasn't so sure.

Maybe I handn't been in the field long enough. Maybe that was why I still had a little compassion left. But it was fading, being worn away like sandstone in a windstorm. A little longer in the field — a week, maybe three — and it would all be gone. I'd be just like the guy who'd killed the little girl's grandmother.

"Do you think that was normal?"

"What?"

"Having lunch next to a dead body."

It sounded like a trick question, a riddle.

"It was normal for Vietnam."

Ellen let the words echo back at me.

"A lot of what you'd told me was normal for Vietnam, wasn't it? Do you think people would have acted that way, done those things if they weren't in Vietnam?"

"No, I guess not."

"Would you sit next to a dead body, have lunch and think nothing of it now?"

"Of course not."

"Would you watch a twelve-year-old having his ear cut off and have no reaction?"

"That's ridiculous."

"So a lot of it had to do with the situation, didn't it? Didn't most of it happen because of the insanity of the place?"

I pushed myself back into the chair and looked up toward the ceiling.

"You know what, Ellen?"

"What?"

"I guess when there's no love, people go insane. Can it be that simple? Do you think that's what it comes down to?"

"Maybe."

"I think Hell must be like that, Ellen. I think Hell must be just like Vietnam . . ."

Chapter Twenty-Four

"The Blessings Tree"

I was sitting on a picnic bench under a maple tree in Fairmount Park. It was warm for early October, but the tree knew winter was coming. Its leaves were just beginning to change.

A few more weeks and it would burst into brilliant color like a fireworks finale . . . a display of contempt for the bitter cold that lay ahead . . . an affirmation that it would survive. It would lay dormant for a while, looking like January had killed it, but it would come back in April stronger than before, better for having lived through the ordeal.

It had been more than a year since I'd finished the Vet Center Program. Somewhere along the way I'd learned that everyone has to deal with alienation, bitterness and disillusionment in their life. It's all around us in the air we breathe and it's part of what it means to be human.

Holocaust survivors, rape victims, people who were abused as children, parents who've lost a child, children who've lost parents, senior citizens who've been abandoned by their families, the physically and mentally handicapped — the litany goes on forever.

You don't have to be a Vietnam Veteran to experience alienation, bitterness and disillusionment. All you need to do is experience life. Everybody's got a "Vietnam."

I'd been volunteering at Norristown State Hospital, playing guitar for the patients once a week. It didn't matter if I was particularly good at it. The patients were being "maintained" on drugs. They wouldn't know the difference.

Many of them had been forgotten by their families. Some hadn't had a visitor in over twenty years. The most powerful anti-depressant in the world can't cure rejection, and I guess seeing someone who cared enough to play the guitar for them helped a little.

When the Interviewing Committee asked me why I wanted to volunteer at a mental hospital, I told them it was to justify Vietnam. I don't think they knew what I meant.

I wouldn't have volunteered if it hadn't been for Vietnam. It taught me what alienation feels like. It made it possible for me to relate to the patients and it made me want to do something to help them. If I could help, then something good would come from it and I thought that might justify it a little.

But there had to be more. There had to be a reason for everything that had happened. I didn't go to Vietnam just to volunteer at a hospital.

I was trying to find the reason for it that day as I sat under the maple tree in Fairmount Park; listening to the silence. It was like being alone in a cathedral.

I thought I knew how to pray, how to say the "Our Father" and "Hail Mary," like reciting poetry. I'd always thought it was strange how "Our Fathers" and "Hail Mary's" worked. You had to say a lot of them, one right after the other. The more you said, the better the chance that one or two of them might actually make it all the way to Heaven. But I didn't need to hear myself recite poetry now. I figured God could see me sitting there on the picnic bench. I figured He knew what had happened to me better than I did, so there was no need to tell Him about it.

I looked up at the blue sky that filtered through the leaves of the tree like sunlight through a stained glass window. Maybe I didn't need to say anything.

"I'll be really quiet, OK? . . . If you're there; if there's something you want to tell me . . . I'm listening."

A minute or two passed and nothing happened. I closed my eyes and tried to make my mind completely blank. A few more minutes passed and I started to feel ridiculous. I glanced at my watch. My lunch break would be over soon.

"Well, if there's nothing . . ."

I got up from the picnic bench and was about to start back toward the office when the leaves of the maple tree suddenly rustled like they were caught in a breeze. The trees on either side of it were perfectly still. It was almost scary.

"If this is supposed to be some kind of sign . . ."

"Whup . . ."

I didn't finish the sentence.

Chills ran up my spine as it came closer. The sound meant "Vietnam." It would always mean "Vietnam."

"Whup . . . Whup . . . WHUP . . . WHUP . . . WHUP . . ."

It was directly over the maple tree now; hovering there like a Medevac looking for wounded on the jungle floor. I shielded my eyes and searched the sky trying to catch a glimpse of it, but I couldn't find it in the bright sunlight.

A moment later, the sound of the Huey's rotors slowly began to fade in the distance . . . a time machine from the past, pausing briefly in the present then continuing its journey into the future.

The leaves of the tree were still again and everything was quiet.

I took the pipe from my suit coat pocket and filled it with tobacco. My hand was shaking as I struck the second match to light it. I took a deep puff and sat down on the picnic bench feeling confused.

I don't know how long I sat there before I heard the silent words. They came from somewhere deep down inside me in a voice that sounded something like my own, but they weren't my words. They were caring and sincere, like a mother's love for her child and they seemed to come just as naturally. I didn't hear them as much as I felt them. . . .

"Feed my sheep, Donnie. . . ."

It startled me. I'd never "heard voices" before. A warm feeling came over me. It was the same way I'd felt when I was seven years old making my first Holy Communion.

Somehow, I knew He wanted me to ask the question now, the question that over the years had retreated to a shadowy recess somewhere deep inside my heart. I looked up through the branches of the maple tree . . .

"Where were you . . . on Easter Sunday?"

I knew the answer before I finished asking the question. . . . He was there on that Easter Sunday in Vietnam.

He was the priest saying the Mass and He was each one of the teenagers sitting around the altar.

He was the Vietnamese boy they'd hung on the tree and the A.R.V.N. interrogating him.

He was the young reporter who's heart broke as he watched everything he believed in being crucified.

He was all of us.

He'd suffered through every moment of Vietnam with me and He'd been there every step of the way on my journey home. He needed to make me see what people do to one another in the total absence of love.

How could I possibly empathize with people who were suffering if I'd never suffered? How could I help people who feel alienated if I'd never been alienated or people who feel bitter if I'd never been bitter?

He needed to have me experience it and He'd helped me to survive like He helps the maple come back to life after a brutal winter. Now He wanted me to "Feed His sheep": use what I'd learned to help other people with the "Vietnams" in their lives.

It was like being given an incredible gift . . . a Master's Degree in Living . . . a "Blessing."

I felt special and humble at the same time, like I'd been chosen. Something good was going to come from Vietnam now. . . . I just knew it!

I'd heard about a group of Vietnam Vets who were meeting in Philadelphia. They called themselves "Vietnam Veterans of America." I'd imagined a bunch of middle aged guys sitting around, blaming their problems on Jane Fonda. I thought the last thing I needed was to join some veterans organization. Now I felt differently. I decided I'd go to the next meeting. Maybe that was where it would all begin.

The meetings were held on the second Wednesday of each month and when I got back to the office, I checked my "Week at a Glance." It had to be more than just coincidence. This was the second week in October. The next meeting was tomorrow night. I felt like Dickens' Scrooge on Christmas morning. I hadn't missed it. There was still time.

The meeting wasn't anything like I'd expected. They came from all walks of life, blue collar, white collar, no collar, and they were trying to accomplish something worthwhile. They were working with orphanages, volunteering a the Veterans Hospital and trying to get the Vietnam Memorial built at Penn's Landing. There wasn't a stitch of camo in the room.

I noticed one of the guys sitting at the front table taking notes. He was the Chapter Secretary and he looked strangely familiar. I pictured his face looking out from under a steel helmet. He was older now, but somehow he seemed like the personification of Vietnam.

Half way through the meeting they introduced me as a new member and asked when I was in Vietnam and what unit I'd served with. When I mentioned the Americal Division, the guy who looked familiar pointed at me.

"I know you!"

I remembered now. I remembered when he got off the chopper and told me about my squad being blown away by the 105. I remembered trying to comfort him as he cried over Goody getting killed. I remembered thinking I'd never see him again.

"Little John? Is that you?!"

He ran over to me and gave me a bear hug. Then he pushed himself back and held me by my shoulders, looking like he was going to cry.

"Welcome home," he said. "Welcome home . . . Brother."

I felt a lump in my throat.

"You too, Little John. . . . Welcome home. . . ."

Two months later I started the Valley Forge Chapter of Vietnam Veterans of America. We collected food to help Mother Theresa care for the homeless and washed cars to raise money to help a kid who has diabetes.

We started a fund for a twelve-year-old boy who has leukemia and we renovated "Mom's House," a free day-care center so unmarried teenage girls can have their babies cared for while they finish high school.

We see to it that kids who are wards of the County have Christmas presents and Easter baskets every year and there are turkey baskets for poor families every Thanksgiving. Everything we do helps people deal with the "Vietnams" in their lives.

The most rewarding experience of all is being asked to visit with high school and college students to tell them what the "Vietnam Experience" was like, and what I learned from it. Being able to do that is one of my greatest blessings from Vietnam.

The students are incredibly interested. Some of their fathers are Vietnam Vets, still unable to talk about it. Some of them just want to know what happened, so much of Vietnam has been blotted out by a national case of "Post Traumatic Stress Disorder."

But I think the students are interested most of all because the Vietnam story is really about them, about what people their age went through and it asks questions they may have to answer for themselves someday.

All I know is that they desperately want to hear the story and like the old sailor in "The Rhyme of the Ancient Mariner"; I desperately need to tell it. . . .

Chapter Twenty-Five

"Brothers"

I arrived at Villanova University earlier than I had to. I wanted to be there when the students filed into the auditorium. I wanted to see their faces, sense why they were there. I had a story to tell them, a story I'd been waiting almost twenty years to tell.

Villanova reminded me so much of Seton Hall — it was like going home again. The students looked like pictures come to life from my college yearbook. I didn't feel older than they were. I felt like I'd been given a chance to go back in time, a chance to tell the nice kid from Seton Hall what Vietnam was going to be like, how he would be disillusioned by it, how it would make him bitter. I wanted to tell him that no one would understand and he would wander through the desert for a long time.

And I wanted to tell him that it would be all right, that Janie would stand by him and he would learn an awful lot from the experience, things he could use to help other people. I wanted to tell him that once he learned how to use it — when he saw the good that would come of it — he'd come to see Vietnam as a blessing.

I wore my best suit and tie. I wanted people to see what a Vietnam Veteran really looked like . . . no camo and no beard . . . no pathetic expression and no "thousand-yard stare."

A warm feeling came over me as I watched the students take their seats. I cared about them, the next generation, and I felt sorry for them too.

There was a stir as a television camera crew walked through the doorway followed by Steve Bell from Channel Three. I'd seen him on television so often, I felt like I knew him and walked over to introduce myself.

"Hello, Steve, I'm Don Yost," I said as I shook his hand.

"Oh, hello."

He looked at me for a long moment like he was trying to remember if he knew me.

"Are you one of the professors?"

"No," I said feeling a little awkward. "I'm one of the Vietnam Veterans."

Steve seemed surprised. He nodded politely as one of the crew members told him it was time to take his place on the stage.

"Where's Jack Kane?" I wondered, hoping he wasn't going to be late.

"Vietnam Veterans are always late. . . ."

I glanced at my watch . . . only ten minutes now. I hoped Jack knew how important this was. If this got on television, it would help the Chapter find other guys who needed us, guys who were still struggling with it.

"Mr. Yost!"

I felt his heavy hand on my shoulder and recognized Jack's booming voice. I turned and looked directly into his broad face.

"Jack! I thought you weren't . . ."

I stopped in mid-sentence.

"What did you do to your hair?!"

It was cropped incredibly short — severe, like a military haircut.

"I always shave it off this time of year."

"In November?!"

"Yeah. In November. Then I don't need a haircut for a few months."

I wished Jack had waited to get his hair cut and I wished he wasn't wearing the camouflaged T-shirt. It accented the huge belly that drooped over his belt. The words "Vietnam Veteran And Damned Proud Of It" were stenciled across it above a map of Vietnam. It made him look like a billboard.

"Is Jeff here yet?" he asked.

"I haven't seen him, but he'd better get here soon. We've only got five minutes."

Dr. Dorley stepped to the podium and adjusted the microphone.

"C'mon, Jack, we'd better get up there."

We took our seats next to Steve Bell, behind the long folding table that was set up on the stage. I looked out at the young faces in the audience. Their eyes stared back at me in silence . . . waiting. They needed to know . . . I could feel it.

A middle aged man in a wheel chair pushed himself slowly down the center aisle. He had no legs. The chair made a squeaking sound as it moved, making everyone turn and look toward him. He finally reached the foot of the stage and sat there for a long moment until one of the students helped him up the ramp.

It was almost one o'clock, the time we were supposed to begin, when Jeff Smith finally stepped onto the stage and took the last seat to my right.

"Boy, it's tough to find a place to park around here. How's it goin' Don?"

"O.K. They're almost ready to start. Did you know Channel Three was going to be here?"

"They said they might show up, nothing definite."

"Well they're here all right."

Jeff was the only guy in the place wearing a baseball cap. He'd pinned a collection of Vietnam badges and ribbons all over it. Somehow, I knew the hat wasn't going to come off.

"Are we ready?" Dr. Dorley asked with his hand covering the microphone. We nodded.

"Good morning," he began. "We have some distinguished guests with us this afternoon. They're going to talk with us about their experiences in Vietnam. As Chair of the History Department, I have my own opinions about Vietnam. I will however, refrain from stating those opinions although it won't be easy for me to do so."

I didn't like the tone of his voice. Dr. Dorley was in his midfifties, too old for Vietnam, but he apparently had strong opinions about it. Maybe he was one of "those people," the ones who'd never been there but thought they knew so much. It had taken me a long time to learn to deal with "those people" and their smug attitude. Maybe I still hadn't learned how to deal with it.

"Let me introduce our guests," he continued. "I think most of you know Professor Quinn of our English Department."

He gestured toward the man with no legs.

"Professor Quinn was a Captain in the Marine Corps and served two tours of duty in Vietnam."

The professor nodded.

"Seated next to professor Quinn are Jeff Smith, Don Yost and Jack Kane of the Vietnam Veterans of America organization and I think you all recognize Mr. Steve Bell of Channel Three. Steve was a Correspondent in Vietnam.

"Well, I'm sure you can take it from here Jeff. I think we're all interested in your opinions of the movie *Platoon.* . . ."

Jeff looked nervous. He reached inside his jacket pocket and found some notes. His voice cracked as he started to read from them.

"Vietnam Veterans of America is a Congressionally Chartered Veterans organization. Our membership is open to Vietnam Veterans and Vietnam Era Veterans and there is also an Associate Membership available."

He was ignoring Dr. Dorley's question. I felt embarrassed for him. Jeff needed some help. I waited until there was an appropriate break in the litany and put my hand on his shoulder.

"May I say something, Jeff?"

"Sure! Go ahead. . . ."

He looked relieved, like he'd been wakened from a nightmare. He pushed the microphone toward me and put the canned speech back in his pocket.

"How many of you have seen *Platoon*?"

Half the audience raised their hands.

"If you haven't seen it you should. It was pretty disgusting, wasn't it? . . . The village burning scene?"

Those who had seen the movie nodded.

"I felt like I'd seen the movie before," I said. "I felt embarrassed by it. *Platoon* isn't just a movie. It shows what I witnessed in Vietnam . . . what I participated in. It tells the truth. . . ."

Professor Quinn's wheelchair squeaked suddenly like the painful cry of a small animal caught in a trap. We were beginning to open the wounds.

"We can't ignore it or try to forget it," I continued. "We have to see what war is like so we don't do it again. Vietnam wasn't about defending Democracy. It was about making a buck!"

The professor couldn't control himself any longer. The words had been suppressed for too long and he fired them into his microphone like an M-16 on full automatic.

"That's what makes America great! You can say whatever you want . . . EVEN IF IT'S NOT TRUE!"

I couldn't see his face. The podium blocked my view. But the tone of his voice, the bitterness in it was unmistakable and familiar.

"The people liked us in Vietnam," he continued. "When we went out on patrol, they would bow down to show us respect. They knew we were there to help them. Look at what happened when we left. . . . Now it's the most suppressed society on the face of the earth!

"I wish we didn't have to waste time talking about *Platoon*. That movie is a disgrace. It dishonors those who gave their lives!"

I'd heard it before in the rap groups I'd been running for Vietnam Vets for the past four years, and I knew where Professor Quinn was coming from. All he had left was the belief that he'd lost his legs for a good reason, and I wasn't going to take that away from him.

There were many things I could have said. I could have told them about the "friendly" village we'd burned, or about the old Papasan they'd killed because he couldn't walk. I could have told them about Easter Sunday and how the screams of innocent children never go away. But I knew I wouldn't tell them. It would hurt too much. I didn't want to feel the pain again and I didn't want to hurt Professor Quinn. After all, he had no legs . . .

A long, awkward moment passed before I spoke again.

"May I say something?"

"I wish you would," Dr. Dorley said.

"What you've just heard is the truth. There is no doubt in my mind that what the Professor told you was his experience. I'm not going to get involved in a debate. All I can tell you is what my experience was and I won't lie about it. There've been enough lies about Vietnam."

Steve Bell leaned toward his microphone.

"Everything you're hearing did happen in Vietnam," he said. "Everyone's experience was different."

"I think we can take some questions now," Dr. Dorley said and hands shot up immediately. He pointed toward a dark-haired girl who was sitting in the second row and she stood up to ask her question.

"How were you treated when you came home?"

Jack grabbed the microphone.

"They called us Baby-Killers. Some Vietnam Vets got spit on! If I ever meet Jane Fonda, I'm going to tell her exactly what I think of her. We call her 'Hanoi Jane.' She should have been put on trial! She's a damned traitor!"

The dark-haired girl took her seat. I wasn't sure she knew about Jane Fonda's trip to Hanoi. She looked confused.

"Most people just didn't want to hear about it," Jeff said. His voice was soft; almost melancholy. "They had blank stares on their faces whenever I tried to talk about it; like I was annoying them. They told me to forget it ever happened, but I can't forget.

"They told us not to wear our uniforms in public when we got home because of the war protesters. Our country was ashamed of us. . . ."

Jeff lowered his eyes. His cap with the badges and ribbons on it didn't seem so out of place anymore.

Another student raised his hand. He had a military haircut that made it obvious he was in Army R.O.T.C.

"I have a question," he said. "Was it because the quality of our troops wasn't what it should have been? Is that why we lost the war?"

"I don't think our Government wanted us to win the war," I answered. "The average age of the kids in the field, the ones actually in combat, was nineteen. Most of them were right out of high school. They were the very best of America's children. . . . The best children America ever wasted."

It was four o'clock when Steve Bell had to leave for another appointment, but the students didn't even seem to notice the TV cameras being turned off.

"We're supposed to finish now," Dr. Dorley said. "But we can stay and continue if you'd like."

No one left the auditorium. Instead, they raised their hands to ask more questions and it was almost seven before Dr. Dorley thanked us for coming and ended the seminar.

I walked across the stage to Professor Quinn. As I approached his wheelchair, he smiled up at me and extended his hand.

"Brothers?" he asked.

"Brothers!" I answered and leaned down to hug him.

I had a good feeling as I pulled out of Villanova's parking lot. I've always felt that way after a school presentation. It's a warm, honest feeling, something like love, but it's also a frustrating feeling. I wasn't able to tell them the whole story; there just wasn't enough time.

I wanted to tell them that everybody's got some kind of "Vietnam" in their life; those things that make us feel alienated, bitter and angry. I wanted to tell them that our "Vietnams" can help us to grow if we let them.

Vietnam Veterans needed to hear the rest of the story too: guys like Jack Kane who were still mad a Jane Fonda, guys like Jeff Smith who still felt like losers and guys like Professor Quinn who were still in denial.

They needed to know how special they were, how much good they could accomplish if they applied the anger in positive ways, if they used it to help other people.

But most of all, I wanted to tell my daughter Michele and my son Dave what I'd learned.

"How are you going to do that?" I asked myself as I pulled into our driveway and shut off the car's engine. "I guess that's why people write books."

I sat there alone in the dark, thinking about it for a moment. . . .

"Maybe I'll call it . . ."